Rick's Hearing Ears

by

Eve J. Peirce

This novel was originally written in the 1990's. Vibrating cell phones and texting, which are now widely available, have made alerting to the phone a less needed skill for hearing dogs trained today.

This is a work of fiction. Names, characters, businesses, places, events and incidents are either the products of the author's imagination or used in a fictitious manner. Any resemblance to actual persons, living or dead, or actual events is purely coincidental.

FridayandFriendsPublishing@gmail.com

ISBN-13: 978-1514898536
ISBN-10: 1514898535

Printed in the U.S.A

Dedication

I would like to dedicate this book to my amazing husband, my family and friends, Dr. Fiorillo, Nurse Melody, Nurse Kerry and the wonderful people at WVCI, Linda S, Lori, Joyce, Robbee, Valeria, Nancy and the other counselors, staff, and supervisors I am lucky enough to work with every day. Your support and kindness helped me get through a very difficult year, and I will always be grateful.

CONTENTS

Chapter		Page
1	Rick..	1
2	The Training Center	9
3	Training Begins	13
4	Rick Gives a Demonstration	21
5	One Month Evaluation	29
6	A Weekend at Sue's House	38
7	Will Rick Learn to Play	44
8	The Mall	52
9	A Decision is Made	61
10	Rick Goes to Dallas	66
11	Cynthia	72
12	Training with Cynthia	82
13	Rick On His Own	90
14	Will Rick Get Washed Out?	97
15	School Demonstration	101
16	Rick Goes to New York	105
17	Robin, Rick, and Randy	112
18	A New Home	124

Chapter One
Rick

Rick looked out through his cage at the people walking up and down the aisle of barking dogs. He longed for a pat on the head or a kind word, and he hopefully watched as each person moved down the row of cages toward his. Would this person talk to him? Would they let him out of the cage? He had seen several dogs leave the building that morning with laughing children or a smiling adult. Would that happen to him today?

Rick had been living alone in his cage for several days now. He had dogs on both sides of him for company, but he longed for his soft bed at home and the happy family he had lived with since he was a puppy. He didn't know where he was or if his family would come back for him. A nice man gave him some food every day and cleaned out his cage, but he was not like the people he had lived with. The man didn't pet him or speak to him very much; he just cleaned, fed and left.

Rick walked to the front of his cage for a better view of the aisle-way. Two little girls and their mother suddenly appeared in front of his door. "Oh, look at this pretty dog, Mommy!" the shorter girl squealed. Rick jumped up and down and wiggled at the attention. The taller girl then stuck her hand through the fencing of his cage and patted him softly on the head. Rick leaned against the hand and wagged his tail.

"Look, Mother," said the girl. "He likes me."

The mother bent over to get a better look at Rick and said, "I don't know. He does seem nice . . . but he's a very big dog."

"Oh, please," cried the girls.

The mother tried to avoid Rick's and her daughters' pleading eyes as she said, "No, I don't think so. We need a smaller dog; he's just too large for our house. Let's look at the dogs on the other side." Rick sadly watched them leave.

Later in the morning two young women wearing dark coveralls walked into Rick's building. They seemed very businesslike as they quickly made their way down the double line of cages, glancing at each dog and then reading the card that hung on each kennel door. Rick heard some of their comments:

"This one is too young--only five-months old."

"This one is just the right size, but it seems afraid of me."

"Here's a friendly little dog, but he doesn't seem very healthy."

"Hey, did you see the terrier?"

"Yes, but it growls."

Rick waited anxiously for them to come to his cage. Eventually, the first woman made her way to his cage. "Sue, come and see this one," she called. Then after reading his card she announced, "Never mind; he's too old."

The second girl came anyway and smiled at Rick. "I like him," she said. "I don't think he's more than a year and a half; let me check his teeth." The next thing Rick knew, his door opened, a collar was slipped over his head and a hand was opening his mouth. "Yep, he's OK," said Sue.

The first girl looked critically at him and said, "I don't know . . . He looks too big."

Sue responded, "Well, we can use a few large dogs, and he really seems friendly. I'm going to take him outside and see how he does." The first girl nodded and then continued her walk down the aisle.

Sue pushed the door to his cage all the way open and stepped out of the way. Rick started to dash out past the girl, but suddenly he felt a tight jerk around his neck. He stopped and looked back to see what had happened. Sue was holding the end of a long leash and the other end was attached to his collar. Rick made a few more attempts to race out the door, but each time he was stopped.

Finally Rick sat down; he was confused. Sue walked up to him and loosened the collar around his neck. She spoke softly to him and patted him on the head. "I guess you haven't learned to heel on a leash," she said. "Just walk with me and the leash won't pull on you."

Sue said, "Let's try again," and patted her leg while giving a small tug on the leash. Rick tentatively stood up and took a few steps. He received a lot of petting and "Good Boy's" for his effort. Rick took a few more steps, staying very close to the girl's leg. Again he was praised. Rick felt he had figured out what he was supposed to do. Sue wanted him to walk next to her. Rick was very pleased that he was now doing what the woman wanted.

Soon they had walked all the way down the aisle, and Sue opened the outside door. When Rick saw the big expanse of green grass outside the opening door, he started to run. Almost before he started, he felt that jerk at his neck and remembered that he was supposed to be walking with the girl. He obediently slowed down and walked carefully with Sue out into the sunshine.

While Rick practiced heeling with Sue, he saw that the other woman had come outside too, and she had a little black dog with wiry, curly hair with her. Rick recognized the dog as Mickey, a friendly dog from across the aisle. Mickey was not fighting with the leather lead and seemed to know all about walking on a leash.

Rick felt a tug at his collar and realized that he had not been watching Sue very carefully. She had turned and he hadn't. Rick raced over to her side. Sue called out to the other girl, "Hey Jane, throw me some toys." Several shapes came flying over to Sue. She caught two and the third, a yellow duck, landed with a squeak as it hit the ground. The toys quickly disappeared into Sue's already bulging pockets.

"Rick, what's this?" Sue asked. Rick looked up and saw that she had a tennis ball. Sue teased him with it a moment and then threw it a short distance. Rick sat and watched the ball land. He was interested in the ball but made no move to pick it up. Sue tried again, but Rick still just watched. Rick wasn't sure what he was supposed to do, but felt that he was not pleasing his new friend.

Sue then reached into her pocket and pulled out the squeaky duck. She squeaked it at Rick and then tossed it in front of him. Rick nosed the duck to see what it was. "Good Boy, Rick. You get that duck," said Sue. Rick wagged his tail a little and looked up at the trainer. Sue tossed the duck for him again, but he just watched it land in the grass. Rick then walked with Sue over to where Jane was working with Mickey.

"How's she doing?" asked Sue.

"She's doing great," Jane answered. "She already knows some obedience and loves to play. Watch this." Jane tossed a toy carrot in the air and Mickey grabbed it before it hit the ground. The dog then tossed it in the air a few times for herself and pounced on it.

"She looks pretty good," said Sue. "She doesn't look nervous and seems to like people . . . and other dogs," she added, seeing that Mickey and Rick were sniffing each other in a friendly fashion.

"How about Rick?" asked Jane. "Are we going to take him too?"

"I'm not sure," said Sue slowly. "He doesn't seem to play and is a little hesitant about things. But I like how he tries so hard to please me, and he has such a good temperament . . . I guess we'll give him a try," Sue said, coming to a decision.

After waiting in front of a high counter while the girls signed some papers, Rick and Mickey were led back outside to a large van. Sue climbed into the back of the van and called to Rick while still holding onto his leash. Rick took a few steps back and then jumped into the van. Sue gave him a little piece of food and closed him into a small cage. Sue told him that he was going for a ride to his new home and not to worry. Rick was happy to be going away and hoped he would soon be taken to his old home.

During the journey in the van, Rick was trying to figure out exactly what was going on. He had been driven from his home to the place with all the cages and barking dogs and then left there for several days. Then today, this new girl in coveralls had let him out of the cage and had attached a leash to his collar so that he had to walk with her. Later she had thrown a ball and a plastic duck and had wanted him to do something with them. Now he found himself in a smaller cage being driven somewhere again. Rick was very glad that Mickey was there, too. He decided that Mickey was not enjoying the ride, as she had gotten sick and was curled up in a miserable little ball.

After driving for a while the van turned sharply and then stopped. Rick heard a lot of activity going on outside. He heard dogs barking, a lawn mower running, and lots of voices.

"Did you all bring back any new dogs?" one voice asked.

Sue answered, "Yeah, we found two at the humane society and two at the dog pound." Sue added after slamming her door shut that the ones from the dog pound--a sheltie and a dachshund, couldn't be picked up until the next day.

Sue and Jane took Mickey and Rick out of their cages, led them into a large, grassy fenced area, and took off their leashes. Rick was so happy to be out of his cage and on grass! He ran in big circles and let out a few joyous barks. Sue, Jane, another woman and a young man, all in coveralls, watched them over the fence. Mickey staggered around for a while and then lay down.

"OK," said Jane, "who's going to work with these new dogs?"

The new woman, who was fairly short with fuzzy brown hair, said, "I need another dog, but I don't care which one."

"I'd like to have Mickey," Jane said. The other three looked at the unhappy little black lump lying on the grass and said that would be fine.

"Do you want Rick?" the young man asked.

"I know you need another one, Jamie," answered Sue, "so you can work with him if you want to."

Jamie watched Rick, who was standing close to Sue, and Sue, who was looking down at Rick, and said that he'd take one of the dogs that would arrive tomorrow.

"I'd like the dachshund," said the shorter woman.

Jamie responded, "That's sounds fine, Kathy. I'll work with the sheltie."

Everyone (including Rick and Mickey) seemed pleased at how the new dogs had been divided. Mickey was soon feeling better and trotted over to Jane, while Rick lay at Sue's feet.

Chapter 2
The Training Center

Rick had been living at this new place for almost a week. Again he had found himself living in a cage, but somehow this time he didn't mind so much. His cage was large and had a wooden bed built into the wall. The bed was just the right height to jump up onto, and he could stay dry up there when the cages were being cleaned. Just below the bed was a door covered by a piece of black rubber. He had found that if he pushed on the rubber, it would open and he could go outside. Outside was much like the inside with a cement floor and walls, but it was nice to be able to lie in the sun.

Sue came to see Rick every day. She fed him in the morning and took him out for a walk in the afternoon. Today Sue took him to the grassy fenced area where he had played the day he had arrived. She put on his leash and said, "Heel." Rick had learned by now that heel meant to walk next to her. He couldn't walk faster or slower or stop to lie down; he had to stay exactly even with her left leg. Sue made a quick turn and sped up, but Rick was watching that left leg and turned at the same time and trotted to keep up. Sue reached down and ruffled his hair. "Good Boy," she laughed. "I can't trick you, can I?"

Next Sue had Rick sit, which he already knew how to do, and then told him to "Stay." Each time Rick tried to get up from sitting, Sue put him right back telling him to sit and then to stay. Finally Rick started to realize that he had to keep sitting and stay still. Each time he stayed, Sue would give him a little piece of cheese. Yum! This was fun!

Then came the thing Rick dreaded. Each day after they had walked awhile, Sue would reach into a pocket and pull out something and want him to do something with it. Yes, there went that hand into a pocket. Sue now had a ball in her hand. "Get the ball, Rick," she said as she rolled it right to his feet. Rick looked down at the ball. He looked at Sue. "Oh, Rick," cried Sue. "Why won't you play?"

Rick didn't understand, but he knew that Sue was not happy. "OK, how about a squeaky shoe?" *Squeak, Squeak* went the toy shoe. Sue put it in Rick's mouth and patted him. "Good Boy with the toy in your mouth," said Sue softly while she stroked his head.

Rick liked being petted but didn't want a hard shoe in his mouth. He dropped the shoe and was sorry that then the stroking stopped. Sue told Rick that he would have to learn to play if he wanted to stay here. "Don't worry," she told him. "On Monday you move up to the main kennels and the real training starts. You'll learn to play then."

Rick was put back into his cage. He was lonely when Sue left. He wanted so much to live in a real home again and have people who would love him and spend time with him. He wasn't unhappy here, but he wasn't quite happy either. Sue's visits were the bright spots in his day.

One morning a few days later, Sue came, but instead of feeding him she put on his leash and walked him over to a big, gray building. He had seen the building the day he arrived but had never been near it. As they approached, he heard lots of dogs barking. Sue opened the door, led him into the building and then put him into a cage quite like the one that he had left.

Rick saw and heard lots of dogs barking and jumping up against their cage doors. It was all very loud and confusing for Rick and he shrank against Sue's legs. Sue patted him on the head and set his food up on the bed. Rick tried to ignore the other dogs. He jumped up on his bed to eat, but it was so loud and he was in a new place, and . . . he just couldn't eat much.

A few minutes later the door to his cage suddenly opened. Rick looked up to see Mickey bouncing into the cage and Jane closing the door after her. Rick jumped off his bed and ran to greet her. Rick was very relieved to see his little black friend. Together they finished Rick's food and then curled up to take a nap on the bed. Rick had been pleasantly surprised to find that this bed

had a foam mat on it, which was very soft. He sighed as
he leaned up against Mickey.

Chapter 3
Training Begins

This is much better than the other place, decided Rick. He and Mickey had just come in from running in the grassy, fenced area with two other dogs. The other dogs had been friendly and they had run and played for quite awhile. One of the dogs, a white and brown spaniel, had found a piece of cloth with a knot in the middle and had run in fast circles. All the other dogs had chased her, and at one point Rick had grabbed the cloth from her.

Jamie, the young man who was often smiling, had made quite a fuss over that. He had rushed over and petted Rick and told him what a wonderful dog he was for getting the tug-of-war. Jamie then picked up the dropped rag and teased him with it by holding it close to his mouth and then jerking it away. Rick just watched him. But, when Jamie gave the tug-of-war back to the spaniel, Rick quickly gave chase and got it again. Jamie talked excitedly to Rick and petted him a lot. All too soon it had been time to go back inside.

Later that afternoon, Rick opened his eyes to see Sue looking at him through his door. The other dogs had barked at her approach and had woken him up. "What are you doing taking a nap when it's time to learn some new things?" laughed Sue. She opened the door, fastened on his leash and led him out of the building. Rick remembered to heel just in time and Sue patted him.

Rick looked around as they walked. He saw several buildings straight ahead, a little building to the right, and a wide parking lot. Rick could see several cars and vans lined up in the parking lot, including the van he had arrived in. Rick wondered what all the buildings were for.

After walking part way across the gravel parking area, Sue turned right and walked up to the little building standing by itself. It looked like a small house and was surrounded by a nice lawn with rose bushes growing near the front door. Sue opened the door and, when they were inside, took off his leash and walked over to a couch.

Rick surveyed the room. Other than the couch that Sue was sitting on, there were also several chairs, a small table, a bookcase and a desk. At the back of the large room he saw a kitchen area with a table and chairs. Rick noticed that Jamie was sitting behind the desk, so he walked around the desk to say hello. Jamie was busy writing in a black notebook, but his writing paused as Rick came up to him.

"Hey Rick," he said, "we're going to have to start filling out a training book for you. Hey Sue, have you filled out Rick's medical history chart yet?"

"Yeah, it's at the back of the book," answered Sue.

"OK, here we are," Jamie said after finding the correct page. He began to read: "Name--Rick, age--1 ½ years, sex--neutered male, breed--Australian shepherd cross, color . . . Let's see, what color are you?" Sue came over to the desk too, and they both looked at Rick.

"He's sort of gray with black spots," said Sue.

"The spots on long hair sure look interesting." Jamie said, "I think his coloring is called blue something . . . I'll look it up to make sure." He pulled a book out of the short bookcase next to the desk.

"He sure is a beautiful dog," said Sue. "Now if this beautiful dog can learn to work sounds and play, we'll have something."

"Oh! Hey! I forgot to tell you," exclaimed Jamie. "Rick was playing with the tug-of-war out in the running area. He wouldn't take it from me, but he sure grabbed it away from Windy. He took it from her twice. I praised him a lot for it; I hope he knew why. I'll write that in his training notes."

Sue was very interested in the news. "Great," she said, "at least there is **something** he will play with."

"I found it," announced Jamie. "He's a blue merle." Jamie read from the book he was holding: "Blue Merle - a common Australian shepherd coat patten." Jamie then began writing again.

While Jamie was busy at the desk, Sue had gotten a can out of a cabinet at the far end of the room. She opened it and Rick suddenly smelled something good. Rick trotted over to her. "Would you like some of this yummy canned dog food?" asked Sue. "You'll have to earn it." She put the can on a shelf located just above a telephone table.

Suddenly the phone rang! It was a very loud ring and Rick looked toward the sound. "Good Boy," Sue said, "let's go see what that is." She hurried toward the phone, so Rick hurried too. When they reached the phone, Sue reached up and got the canned food from the shelf. "Up here, Rick," she said, holding the can above the table. Rick stretched his head toward the food. Sue held it higher. Rick put his front feet on the low table which held the ringing phone so he could reach the food. Sue gave him a big spoonful and a big hug. "What a good boy you are," she sang. "When the phone rings you get some food. Isn't that easy?"

Sue put the can back on the shelf and moved a short distance from the phone. Rick went with her and waited to see what would happen next. So far he was enjoying himself. It was fun to come to this new building and be fussed over and fed good things.

The phone rang again. Rick looked at Sue. "Let's go," said Sue. Rick bounded over to the table and found some food already there. It was on the back edge of the table, so again he had to put his front paws on the table to reach his treat. Sue followed him over and pet him for a long time at the phone. Rick wagged his tail back and forth.

They repeated the whole process several times and, by the end, Rick had discovered that he would get food every time he ran to the table after the phone had rung. He had tried going to the table when the phone hadn't rung, but there was nothing there. What a fun game! I hope we can do this again, thought Rick.

Over the next few days Rick learned that he would get food not only at the phone, but also at the oven when the timer rang and at the door when the doorbell rang.

A few days later Rick was in the training apartment again, relaxing after practicing a few sounds with Sue. "Today," said Sue, "we're going to teach you the other half of your job." Rick looked at Sue with expectation. He was enjoying his training sessions in the little building and wondered what he would learn today.

Rick noticed that Jane was sitting behind the desk today. He wasn't sure why there was always someone there at the desk, but he thought it had something to do with the sounds. Several times he had seen Jamie reach up and click something just before the phone rang.

Buzz! Buzz! went the doorbell. Rick jumped to his feet and ran to the door. He looked back to see where Sue was. She was sitting in one of the chairs. Why wasn't she following him? Rick jumped up and down at the door. Just then Sue called "Rick, come here." Rick ran back to the chair where Sue was sitting. "Up here, Rick," said Sue. She was patting her lap and holding a spoon of canned food in front of her.

Rick hesitated. He had been taught by his earlier family not to jump on people, and here Sue was calling him up to her lap. He smelled the good food and jumped all the way into Sue's lap. Rick got his treat as Sue struggled to hold the large, wiggly dog on her legs. Soon Sue pushed Rick gently off, and he jumped back onto the floor.

"I guess we'd better practice this a few times," Sue laughed. "I don't want you all the way on my lap, just your front feet. Let's try again without any sound."

Rick was sitting on a rug next to the chair looking puzzled. He could hear Jane laughing over at the desk. Somehow he knew that he hadn't done quite the right thing.

Rick heard Sue calling to him again. This time she was holding the spoonful of food just above her knees. Rick reached toward the spoon, but he couldn't quite reach it. "It's OK, Rick," said Sue patting her knee. Rick finally put a paw on her knee so that he could reach that yummy food (it was chicken today). Sue fed him and reached down and picked up his other foot and put it on her other knee. "Good Boy, Rick," she said ruffling his hair with both hands. She said lots of "good boy's and Rick soon relaxed and began to enjoy himself. After a few minutes Sue set his front feet back on the floor.

Rick sat at attention watching Sue. "Here, Rick," called Sue, patting her knee again. Rick quickly put his front feet on her knees and was rewarded with a different kind of treat. It was a chewy, meaty square piece of food. Yum! Several more times Sue called Rick to her and each time he jumped up and received some attention and something to eat.

"OK, Jane, " said Sue. "I think he's ready to try hitting me with a sound. Would you ring the doorbell again?" Getting no response Sue called loudly, "Jane!"

"What!" said Jane, sounding startled. She had been leaning back in her chair with her feet propped up on the desk. As her feet thudded back onto the floor she answered, "Sorry . . . Did you want the doorbell?"

Rick looked up to see Sue laughing this time.

Buzz! Buzz! Rick had been watching Jane again, but now looked at the door. Before he had taken more than a few steps, he heard Sue calling him. He raced over and put his paws on her knees. He barely had time to gobble the treat Sue handed him before he was back on the floor running to the door. This time, Sue followed him there and gave him lots of attention. She clapped her hands as Rick jumped up and down, and then petted and talked to him awhile. They repeated the whole process three more times. Each time the doorbell rang, Rick ran to Sue and then to the door.

"Very impressive," said Jane. "He seems to catch on pretty fast."

"Are you an impressive dog, Rick?" asked Sue. Rick wagged his tail. Rick was pleased with himself and was glad that Sue and Jane were too.

Chapter 4
Rick Gives a Demonstration

Jamie was holding open Rick's door saying, "Hurry up, Rick. You're doing a demonstration, and boy do you need a bath! If we hurry, we'll just have time to get you cleaned up." Rick bounced down a long hallway next to Jamie. He thought maybe they were going outside to play and was surprised when Jamie opened a door into a little room. "OK, up we go," groaned Jamie as he lifted Rick into a waist-high bathtub. Rick struggled, but ended up in the bathtub anyway. "You just sit still and it will be over soon."

Rick didn't like baths. His former family had washed him a few times and he didn't like it. He was happy that Jamie was careful not to get soap in his eyes. Eventually he was pronounced clean and put back on the floor. With a great shake Rick rid himself of most of the water. "Hey!" cried Jamie. "You're getting me all wet!"

Jamie reached into a cabinet and pulled out a big, fluffy towel. Rick did like being dried off and rubbed against the towel, and then against Jamie's legs. Jamie snapped on a leash and walked him over to the training apartment. "Sue will be surprised I gave you a bath," said Jamie. "She's been busy all morning, so I thought I'd save her some time."

As they walked into the apartment, Sue glanced up from some papers she was working on at the desk. "Rick, You've had a bath! Thanks, Jamie; I owe you one."

"No problem," said Jamie. "I had a little time before Jane and I go into town. Hey, are you sure he's ready to give a demo? He's still fairly new."

"Actually, I'm just anxious to see how he'll act around all the people. I'd like to know right away if he's going to have any problems besides not playing."

"I bet he'll do fine," answered Jamie. "He's been working great so far."

"Hey! Jane's leaving for town without me, " Jamie cried while looking out the window. "Wait for me, Jane!" he yelled as he ran out the door.

Now that Jamie was gone, Sue turned her attention back to Rick. First she brushed his damp hair and then had him lie down on a rug near the heater. "Today you're going to show a group of people how hearing dogs work. I hope you don't get nervous with lots of people around."

Rick's hair dried, he was brushed again and then he practiced some sounds with Sue. After they had been working awhile, the doorbell rang. Rick ran to tap Sue and then ran to sit at the door. "Good Boy," said Sue. "Let's see who's here."

When the door opened, ten people trooped in, led by Kathy, the shortest trainer, whom Rick didn't see very often. Kathy introduced Rick and Sue to the group and then asked the people to sit down. It took a few minutes and a few chairs dragged forward from the kitchen area for everyone to find a seat. Rick went from person to person so that everyone could pet him. He enjoyed all the attention he was getting. Each person seemed eager to stroke his head or run a hand along his back.

"Is it OK to pet Rick?" someone asked.

Kathy answered, "Yes, you can pet Rick a little since he's just started his training and needs to get used to being with large groups of people. We want him to enjoy meeting lots of new, friendly people during tours like this one so he'll feel confident when he goes into crowded areas." Kathy added that hearing dogs working with their deaf master at home or in public should be left alone. She explained that other family members are not even allowed to give much attention to a deaf person's dog.

Eventually, Sue called Rick over to her. "You can just lie down and relax, Rick," said Sue. "That's enough petting for you for a while." Rick thought he could use more petting, but he minded and lay down next to Sue's feet.

"I'll let Sue tell you a little about hearing dogs," said Kathy. "Then we'll see if Rick can show you how hearing dogs work sounds." Kathy walked over to the desk and sat down as Sue began to talk.

"We get most of the dogs we train from local humane societies and dog pounds," Sue explained. "We look for dogs that are about six months to a year old, are healthy, like being around people, and like playing with toys. We also try to make sure that they are not aggressive with people or dogs, are not too timid, and are dogs that like to please."

Sue paused and then continued. "A dog with all these qualities is sometimes hard to find, but each requirement is important. We choose young dogs so that they will have more years to help their deaf masters. The reason we must be sure that our dogs are not aggressive or too nervous is because they are allowed by law in all public places. Picking dogs that play is also very important because that is how the dogs are rewarded for working sounds, both here during training and after they are placed with the deaf recipients."

An elderly lady sitting on the couch asked, "Why don't you give them treats instead of toys?"

Kathy walked toward the group and answered, "Most people don't want to keep dog treats in their pockets all the time or keep food next to each sound in the home; it's just easier to use toys." Kathy went on, "There is also the excitement factor. A dog will be more excited about taking you to the phone if he gets to chase a ball one time, a squeaky toy the next, and then sometimes get a nylon bone to chew on. Using toys as a reward is exciting for the dog; he doesn't know which toy he will get, and he will enjoy it longer than a bite of food."

"We do use food initially when we're training the dogs," said Sue, "but we soon switch to toys as rewards. Toys won't make the dog fat and are just easier to use."

"Let's watch Rick work some sounds," Kathy suggested, "and then we'll tell you a little more about the dogs."

Kathy walked back to the desk, and soon Rick heard: *Ring! Ring!*

Rick leapt to his feet. He jumped lightly onto Sue's nearest knee and then ran to the phone. Sue tried to pet Rick as he made contact with her, but he was already gone. She followed him to the phone and said, "Good Boy, Rick. What a very good dog!" She ruffled up his clean hair and gave him a squeeze.

"Why didn't he get a toy?" asked a teenage girl.

"Well," said Sue, "Rick hasn't quite learned to play with toys yet. He will play tug-of-war with the other dogs, but won't play with us."

"How come he was picked out if he won't play?" asked an older man.

"I chose Rick because he is a friendly, happy dog who tries so hard to please me," said Sue. "I'm hoping that he will learn to play because, as you just saw, he is working sounds well and would be a great companion to someone. We'll just have to see if he learns to like toys. If he doesn't, he'll be taken back to the humane society or given to a hearing person as a pet." Sue took a breath and then added, "His one-month evaluation is coming up in a few weeks, and we'll probably decide then whether to keep him in training or not."

"Poor Rick," said the elderly woman. "He looks like he really wants to be a hearing dog. He was so fast to that phone."

Sue replied, "If he is 'washed-out' and has to leave our program, he will probably get to have a family again sooner than if he completes his training. It takes about five to six months to train a hearing dog, and during that time the dogs have to live in the kennels. So . . . Rick might be happier if he doesn't make it."

"Do many of the dogs get 'washed-out'?" the teenaged girl asked.

Kathy answered. "About half of the dogs don't make it for some reason or another. Some are afraid to go to stores and be out in public, some have a health problem, a few turn out to be aggressive, some don't learn to play, and some just aren't good enough at working sounds."

"Well, I think Rick would make a wonderful hearing dog," said the older woman. "I bet he learns to play."

While the woman was talking, Kathy had gone around the corner into the other room. Suddenly she called out, "Sue! Sue!"

Rick jumped up and ran to see where Kathy was. When he got to her, Kathy said, "Go get Sue." Rick dashed back and tapped Sue and then led her back to Kathy.

The people who were watching all smiled and began to clap. Rick trotted back to his audience wagging his tail. He liked having these people watch him work.

Sue came back and sat in her seat. "What we just did is called a Name Call," she explained. "It's a new sound for Rick, and he's caught on pretty fast."

Sue continued after giving Rick an affectionate pat on the head, "The name call is an important sound for a deaf person's family because they can call the deaf person's name and the dog will bring that person to them. This is very useful for children of deaf parents. If the child gets hurt or just needs Mom or Dad, they can send the hearing dog to bring the deaf parent."

Rick was lying down again and began to doze off as Kathy was saying that the dogs cost more than $20,000 to train but are given free of charge to the people that need them.

Rick awoke as the people began to rise from their chairs and walk to the door. He sat near the doorway and let each person pat him on the head as they left. He listened to the kind tone of their farewells:

"What a good dog you are, Rick."

"I hope you won't get washed out, boy."

"You just decide to like those toys and you'll get to go help someone who needs you."

"Good bye, Rick."

Chapter 5
One Month Evaluation

Rick was battling Windy, the Brittany Spaniel, for the tug-of-war out in the fenced play area. They each held on fiercely to one end of the rag and stood with their forelegs resting on the ground and their hind ends high. Suddenly, Mickey dashed in and grabbed the tattered rag in the center, just between the two sets of clenched teeth. Now it was a three-way fight! They ran in crazy circles as each dog tried to pull the cloth free. Finally Windy won and took a triumphant run around the enclosure with her head held high and with the limp rag trailing from her mouth.

Rick laid down in a shady spot and Mickey soon joined him. Rick's tail thumped the ground a few times as he gave Mickey a friendly sniff. He was glad to get to play with his friend outside today. Mickey had been moved to a different cage several days ago, and Rick missed her company.

Nearly every day, Sue or one of the other trainers would let him out into the large fenced area, but it wasn't always with the same group of dogs. Yesterday, when Rick trotted around the play area to see who was there, he rubbed against Hap, a golden cocker spaniel, who was chewing on a bone. Hap had jumped up with a growl and bared teeth and had chased him away. Jamie was the trainer watching them that day, and he had run over and scolded Hap. After that, Rick kept well away from that grumpy dog.

The dogs out today were his old pals: Windy--the very fast spaniel, Maggsy--a fluffy white dog with curly hair, and Mickey. Rick had figured out that these were all dogs Sue took care of, except Mickey who was Jane's.

All too soon, the gate opened and Sue called the dogs back into the kennels. Rick ran in with the rest hoping that Sue would take him to the little building where he practiced sounds. Nope, she put him in his cage, gave him a pat, and took Windy out with her.

Windy and Sue had barely gone out the door when Kathy and Jane walked in. Kathy was holding a clipboard, and she and Jane looked up and down the row of cages as if deciding something. As they walked closer Rick heard Kathy say, "OK, Sue just took Windy over. Who else is up for their one month evaluation?"

Jane answered, "Umm . . . there's Rick, Mickey, Hap, and . . . who else came in just after Hap? Oh yeah, Maggsy."

"How about your two fox terriers, Wally and Dinky?" asked Kathy.

"They better wait till next time, I think," replied Jane. "I've only been working with them about three weeks."

Kathy said, "Then we'll do Mickey after Windy, then Maggsy, then Hap, and last Rick."

"OK," agreed Jane. "We should get them all done this afternoon."

Rick wasn't sure what they were talking about but had wagged his tail both times he'd heard his name.

Later that afternoon, Sue came into the kennel and let Rick out of his cage. Rick heeled all the way to the training building, stopping a few times to sit, as requested.

As soon as they entered the little building, Rick could feel tension in the air. He and Sue stopped just inside the doorway and looked to see what was happening. Kathy, Jane, and Jamie were standing in the center of the room, but no one was talking. Hap was lying on a rug at the far end of the room.

Finally Jamie said, "He's just too possessive with bones and toys. He went nuts yesterday when Rick came close to his bone."

Kathy said, "I really think he's getting better; he's definitely not a washout."

Jane interjected, "I agree with Jamie. I think he's way too aggressive."

Kathy frowned at both of the other trainers and then said, "Why don't I go get a fresh bone and we'll give it to him now that Rick's here."

"Keep him on the leash for a minute, will you Sue?" said Jamie. "We're going to try Hap with a bone."

"I'll go get one," said Kathy, sounding unhappy. "I'll be right back."

Rick sat down near Sue's feet as she sat on the couch. Sue asked the other two what had been decided.

"Kathy wants to keep him in training since he's doing so well with sounds, but we think he's too aggressive," Jane explained to Sue.

Sue remarked, "I haven't seen that side of him recently, but I remember how he used to act on bone day. He'd get pretty frantic about protecting his bone from the dogs in cages next to his." Sue added, "I don't know why so many cocker spaniels are like that."

"Well, we'll see in a minute," said Jamie as they watched the front door open.

Kathy then walked in with a meaty beef bone and went into the next room to give it to Hap. The others watched Hap through a window built into the wall, and saw him happily licking and chewing on the bone. Kathy reached down to take it from him; he passed the test--he let her. "Good Boy, Hap," said Kathy. "OK Sue, let Rick loose and get him to come in here."

Sue unfastened Rick's leash and walked around the corner. Rick followed, but as soon as he saw Hap with a bone he stopped. The smaller dog glanced up at Rick and then the golden dog's hackles rose. Hap stared menacingly at Rick and let out a low, threatening growl.

Rick retreated out of the room as Kathy grabbed Hap's collar.

"Bad Dog! No growling!" Kathy scolded. "OK, I'm convinced. He'll go back to the shelter tomorrow, and I'll tell them about the growling."

As Hap was led out in disgrace, Rick ventured back to the other room and began chewing on the bone. No one spoke for awhile. Finally Jamie said, looking up from a list in front of him: "Mickey and Mags have passed without any trouble, Hap and Windy are washed out, so that just leaves us with Rick."

"Sorry about Windy not making it," Jane said to Sue.

"Thanks," Sue answered, "I really liked her, but . . . she does have a definite energy problem."

Jamie added, "Yeah, She sure worked fast, but she needed a **lot** of exercise."

"I think she'll be happier living with those people in the country who called last week," Sue said. "I'm glad you guys remembered about them. They wanted a well-trained dog for their kids, and she'll be perfect."

Kathy came back saying, "Let's get Rick going so we'll have time to let out the last few dogs before we go home. Who's going to do sounds?"

Jamie volunteered and walked over to sit behind the desk. Rick was contentedly working on the bone when he heard something. He stopped chewing and lifted his head.

Buzz! Buzz!

It was the doorbell. Rick jumped up, screeched around the corner, found Sue, touched her leg with a paw, and then came to a sliding sit at the door. "Good Boy, Rick!" said Sue. The other three applauded his efforts. Even Rick thought he had been very dramatic getting to the sound, and he felt pleased about it.

Jane said, "Wow! Did you see how fast he left the bone?"

"He's really good with all the sounds I've seen," said Kathy. "What problems does he have besides not playing?"

Jamie looked in Rick's training book and read, "Good with people and children during tours, a little nervous in strange places, nervous around traffic, good with other dogs, no housebreaking problems." Jamie concluded, "I guess nervousness is the only other problem he's having. Is that right Sue?"

"Yep," came the reply.

"Have you taken him to town yet, Sue?" asked Jane.

"No, he's only been on a few walks around here," replied Sue. "He seems to enjoy going places with me, like into the office, but is a little hesitant when we walk along the road. I'm not sure if that's something that will get better or not."

Rick worked the telephone when he heard it ring, and then immediately afterwards he heard Jamie call

Sue's name. Rick tapped Sue and then crawled through the kneehole of the desk to sit at Jamie's feet. They all laughed at the sight of the big, gray shape wedged under the desk.

Rick stayed put until Sue and Jamie had each petted him and told him what a good dog he was. Sue found a treat in her pocket for him, too. Only then did he back out from under the desk. He looked questioningly at the four trainers to see if anyone looked likely to set off another sound. Rick decided he was done working for a while and headed back to his bone.

Jamie asked, "Well, what's the consensus on Rick?"

"What do you think, Jane?" asked Kathy.

"Oh, I don't know. He's a good worker and seems to mind well, but he sure won't play . . . "

Jamie piped in, "I think Rick should be given a little more exposure to traffic and new places before we wash him out for being too nervous."

Sue asked, "Well, what do you think, Kathy?"

"I don't think he's the kind of dog we want," came the answer. "We all think he's a nice dog, but he won't play with toys." Kathy continued, "He responds well to attention and verbal praise, but a deaf owner may not be able to speak and probably won't praise him as much at sounds as we do. I think not playing and being insecure are too many strikes against him."

Sue said, "Well, if the rest of you guys agree, I'll

wash him out. But I'd really like to give him a little more time."

"Why don't we keep him around a few more weeks and have Sue really concentrate on getting him to play?" suggested Jamie. "He could also go to town several times so we could see if he'll get used to traffic and going places."

Jane nodded at Jamie's suggestion and said, "I can try bringing him in when I'm playing with Mickey. Maybe seeing his friend playing with me will help. I vote to give him a little longer."

"OK," said Kathy. "It won't hurt to keep him a few extra weeks, but if he still won't play and is nervous in town, he should go."

Sue said as she stood up, "That sounds fair. Well, I guess I'll take him back to the kennel and let the rest of the dogs out." Sue paused, "Maybe I'll take him home with me this weekend and see how he handles working sounds in a new place."

Rick walked back to the kennel building with Sue, carrying the big bone in his mouth. He was unaware that his stay at the training center had only narrowly been extended. As far as Rick was concerned, today had been great. He had received lots of attention when he worked sounds, enjoyed a nice time with Mickey outside, and now had a bone to gnaw on.

As Sue put him in his cage, she stooped down and hugged him. "Oh Rick, you're such a wonderful dog. I sure hope you learn to play."

Chapter 6
A Weekend at Sue's House

It was late on Friday afternoon and Rick could hear the trainers getting into their cars to drive home. He heard Kathy and Jamie discussing a softball game that they would play that evening. Several car-door-slams later, as Rick was settling down to work on his new bone (the dogs were given big, beef knuckle bones on Fridays), the kennel door opened and Sue walked in saying, "Come on, Rick. I'm taking you home for the weekend."

Rick lost no time in bounding out of his open cage and out of the building. Sue opened the back door of her car and told him to jump in. Rick hopped up onto the seat, wagging his tail and feeling very happy. His window was open a few inches, so Rick closed his eyes and let the wind hit him in the face as they drove away. Rick loved to ride in cars and was glad he was going somewhere. Yippee!

Soon Sue turned off the road onto a long driveway. They bumped along slowly and finally stopped in front of a small house. Rick noticed that there was a shady front porch as well as a large front yard. He also saw a big animal out in a field. "This is where I live," said Sue. "I think you'll like it here. Let's go in and meet Annie."

Annie turned out to be a large tan and white collie. She was waiting at the front door when Sue opened it and came bouncing out onto the porch. Rick hesitated a minute as he was inspected by the large, fluffy dog. A few sniffs later the collie began wagging her tail.

Sue was holding open the front door, so Rick went into the house and looked around. He was standing in a long, narrow living room and saw a small kitchen through a doorway to his right. As he sniffed around, he found a water dish and some crumbs on the kitchen floor. Eventually he settled down on the living room carpet and stretched out. This was a good place, Rick decided. Sue was here and the whole house smelled pleasantly of dog.

A few hours later someone knocked on Sue's front door. Rick looked up at Sue, who was sitting nearby on a sofa, to see if he should be responding. He was used to working in the training apartment, but he had never worked sounds anywhere else. "Come on, Rick," said Sue. That was all it took. Rick put his paws on her knees and then ran and sat at the door.

"Good Boy, Rick!" exclaimed Sue. "That was very good." When the door opened, Rick saw a tall young man with dark wavy hair standing there. "Hi, Todd," said Sue, giving him a kiss. "Come on in and meet Rick."

"Well, so this is Rick," said Todd. "I've heard a lot about you." Todd scratched Rick behind the ears and then gave some attention to Annie who had pushed her way through.

"Would you mind doing a few more door knocks for us?" asked Sue. "And please take Annie out with you. She's getting in the way."

Todd good-naturedly agreed and called Annie as he retreated out the door. Sue walked through the living room and went back into the bedroom and lay on the bed. Rick followed and lay down on the floor. They both lay still, waiting for something to happen. Rick knew that he would hear a sound soon. There it was. He heard a knocking at the door. He ran to the door to make sure where the sound was coming from and then ran back to tap Sue. Soon they were both at the door and Todd and Annie were coming back in.

"How did he do?" asked Todd

"He was perfect," said Sue. "I was lying on the bed and he tapped me on the first try. We've just started working on that type of hit." Sue ruffled Rick's hair and thanked Todd for the knocks. "I don't think we need any more. He was waiting for that one. Why don't you sit down and relax? I was just going to bake some cookies." Todd's face lit up at the mention of cookies.

After all the excitement of Todd's arrival and working some sounds, Rick settled back down to take a nap on the soft living room rug. Rick could see Sue busily working on something in the kitchen, Todd reading on the couch, and Annie's legs sticking out from under the kitchen table. Rick soon drifted off to sleep.

Suddenly he awoke with a start. Something was ringing! Rick leaped to his feet. Where was Sue? Where was the sound coming from? He looked around quickly and found Sue sitting on the couch beside Todd. He ran over, touched her knee with a paw, and ran toward the sound. The buzzing was coming from the oven, and boy, did something smell good. Rick collided with Annie, who had come out from under the table to see what was going on, as he came to a sliding stop in front of the stove.

Rick was so proud of himself for going to this new sound. He bounced up and down, wagging his tail while he waited for Sue to come and praise him. Sue had followed him to the stove and said "Rick, sit." In his excitement, Rick had forgotten to sit down! He quickly sat.

Sue said, "What a good boy, Rick. What do I have to give such a good dog?" Sue reached up on top of the stove and handed Rick a great big dog biscuit. She continued to tell him what a good dog he was while she opened the oven and took out the wonderful smelling things.

"Thanks for coming to get me, Rick," said Sue. "I'm glad I set the oven timer, because I forgot it was time to take them out. You won't let me forget, will you?" While Sue was talking, Annie came over and sniffed at the biscuit that Rick was eating. Sue gave her a biscuit, too.

As Sue lifted the cookies off the cookie sheet, she explained to Todd that deaf people who had hearing dogs weren't allowed to have any other dogs. "It's just not fair for the person to divide their attention between the hearing dog and a family pet. The hearing dog has to work every time he hears a sound, and he deserves all the praise and attention his owner can give him."

Sue carried in a hot cookie to Todd saying, "If the owner doesn't have a great relationship with his hearing dog, the dog won't want to do his job." Todd looked at Rick and Annie eating their snacks and said, after he had taken a bite of the chocolate chip cookie, "I guess it really isn't fair for both dogs to be rewarded equally, when Rick was the one who was working."

After a wonderful weekend of playing with Sue and Annie, and meeting the big, brown animal in the field (Sue called it Simon and rode on its back both afternoons), and learning some new sounds, and sleeping on a soft rug during the day and on a fluffy bed with Annie at night, it was time to leave. Sue was holding open the car door and motioning for Rick to jump in. He got in and looked back at the house as they drove away. Rick wished he could just stay at the little house and live with Sue and Annie.

When the car stopped Rick knew he was back at the training center. He could hear his friends barking, and smell the familiar smells. Soon he was back in his kennel again. He suddenly felt very lonely. He hoped Sue would come to see him soon. Rick leaned against the kennel door and wished that he had a real home.

Chapter 7
Will Rick Learn to Play?

Rick wasn't left in his cage very long that morning. Jane soon came to let Mickey out and then opened his door too. The dogs were happy to see each other, and Jane had a hard time making her way to the outside door amidst the wagging tails and bouncing bodies.

Finally, they were all three outside and on their way to the training building. Neither dog was on a leash, but they both stayed close to Jane. Jane told them to sit when they came to the door. Rick and Mickey sat down simultaneously. "Stay," Jane commanded as she opened the door. Neither dog moved, but their eyes went back and forth between Jane and the inviting open door. Finally Jane released them with an, "OK"

Rick and Mickey bounded into the training apartment. Mickey spotted a squeaky carrot lying on the floor and pounced on it. *Squeak! Squeeeeeak!* went the plastic carrot. Rick looked on interestedly. Jane snatched the carrot away from Mickey and teased her with it. Mickey jumped and tried to reach the toy that was held just out of her reach. Jane tossed the carrot towards the far side of the room and Mickey was instantly in motion.

After Mickey chomped on the toy a few times, Jane took it from her and showed it to Rick. "Hey, Rick!

Wouldn't you like to play with this carrot?" Jane asked. "Here, try to grab it." Jane held the carrot out to Rick and then hid it behind her back. "Where's the carrot? Oh, here it is," she said holding it out again. Rick sniffed at the carrot but didn't try to take it. "OK Rick, I'm going to let Mickey have it." Mickey grabbed the toy and ran into the other room.

The front door opened and Sue came in. "How's it going with Rick?" she asked.

Jane answered, "Mickey's having fun and Rick is getting kind of excited, but so far he hasn't picked up any toys."

"Let's try the tug-of-war," suggested Sue. "I've got one here in my pocket.

"Rick, Mickey, look what I have," Sue called in an inviting voice. Mickey ran in from the other room and tried to grab the rag hanging from Sue's hand. Sue held it above her reach and then teased Rick with it.

Rick looked at the blue rag. He wasn't sure what he was supposed to be doing with it. All of a sudden the knotted rag was gone. Mickey had it and was trotting away from him! Rick quickly caught up with her and tried to bite at the tug-of-war. Mickey spun around, trying to hold the rag out of his reach. Rick, who was much taller, had no trouble reaching the rag, and he grabbed the long end. The two dogs held onto their ends and tugged at each other. Rick pulled and pulled and

. . . finally pulled the blue cloth free. Rick felt very happy with himself. He galloped around the room with Mickey close at his heels. A few seconds later he heard Sue calling him so he trotted over and sat down at her feet, still holding the rag.

"What a good boy!" exclaimed Sue. "What a very good dog." Sue ruffled up his hair as she talked to him. "Can I take that tug-of-war?" she asked while reaching for its end. Rick dropped the rag when he felt her holding on to it. "Here, Rick, try to get it." Sue dangled the rag in front of him and then quickly pulled it back.

Rick followed the soggy, blue rag with his eyes. He wanted to grab it, but something held him back. He could see the disappointment in Sue's eyes as he sat there. What was he supposed to do? Why was Sue happy when he had the rag, and unhappy when he didn't?

Sue held the rag out to Mickey. Mickey didn't hesitate; she took hold of the rag and tried to pull it out of Sue's hand. Sue didn't let go. She held on and laughed at Mickey's pretend fierce attack on the rag. Then Sue held out her end to Rick. The rag bounced back and forth with each of Mickey's tugs. Rick could sit still no longer. He sank his teeth into the end Sue was holding, being careful not to touch her hand.

"Good Boy, Rick! Sue exclaimed.

"Hey, Jane did you see how he took the rag from me?" Sue asked excitedly. Rick and Mickey were again in battle for the cloth. This time Mickey won. She surrendered the rag to Jane when asked, but watched attentively for a chance to take it again.

Jane held the rag out to Rick. "Here you go, Rick. Come and get it." Rick came over to Jane but didn't reach for the rag. "OK, if you don't want it I'll give it to Mickey," Jane warned. She held the tug-of-war above the two dogs' heads. Mickey jumped in the air trying to reach the rag. Rick just looked up. Mickey tried again, this time almost getting it. Rick tried this time too. He had the advantage because of his size and took the rag gently from Jane's hand.

"Good Boy!" came two voices. Jane stroked Rick as Sue hurried over to them. Sue then reached in her pocket and pulled out a little meaty treat. Rick dropped the rag to eat his reward. He gobbled up the tiny treat and happily wagged his tail as the two girls praised him.

"Maybe he is gonna play, " said Jane. "At least he likes the tug-of-war."

"Yeah," agreed Sue. "This is a start, anyway." As Sue walked over to the desk and began writing, Jane asked how Rick had done over the weekend.

"He was very good," answered Sue. "He worked the doorbell and oven buzzer real well, even when Annie got in his way. He wasn't afraid of Todd, or of being in a strange house either."

"What did he think of the horse?" Jane asked.

"Well, he was a little nervous when Simon sniffed him, but he didn't try to run away or anything." Sue continued, "I left him and Annie on the front porch a few times while I was riding, and he was very good about staying. Annie wandered off once or twice, like she tends to, but he stayed put."

"That's good to hear," said Jane. "Are you going to take him to town this week?"

"I thought I'd take Maggsy later in the week, like Thursday, but I'm not sure about Rick," answered Sue.

Kathy's face appeared at the window in the front door. "Do you want a door knock before I come in?" came her muffled voice.

"No," came the joint reply from Sue and Jane.

As Kathy came into the room, she saw the two dogs and asked, "Been trying to get Rick to play?"

Sue answered, "Yeah, he's getting more interested in the tug-of-war; he took it from us twice."

"Nice," responded Kathy vaguely. "Are you two finished? I want to work my dogs before lunch."

Jane and Sue decided that they were finished with the playing session and took Rick and Mickey outside on leashes to practice obedience.

Over the next few days, it became a new routine that either Sue or Jane would take Rick and Mickey to the training building or out into the running area to play tug-of-war. Rick was beginning to figure out that he would be petted and fussed over if he picked up the blue, knotted rag. He liked grabbing it away from Mickey or trying to pull it out of the trainer's hand, and he liked getting praised for it too.

Rick now knew what to do with knotted rags, but he still didn't understand what he was supposed to do with the funny, hard, plastic shapes. He saw that Mickey liked to bite at them and throw them around, but he didn't think that was fun. He didn't like having the hard toys put into his mouth, and he didn't ever try to take them away from Mickey. He knew this disappointed Sue and Jane, but he just didn't like those toys.

Today, Rick was practicing alerting Sue to the sound of a baby crying. Whenever he heard the crying sound, he had to find Sue, take her into the other room, and then sit down next to the crib. That was fairly easy, but this time Sue wasn't sitting or lying down; she was walking around the room. Rick could hear the crying sound, but he couldn't seem to jump up at the right time to touch Sue's leg. Every time he jumped up, she had moved. Why didn't she hold still?

"Come on, Rick," Sue called out invitingly. "If you can tap me, you can have this treat." She held a spoonful of canned dog food down near his nose, and then raised it back up to just below her waist.

Rick wanted that food! He tried to jump at the right time, and this time he touched her. Sue stopped and fed him his reward with his front feet still leaning against her. "What a good boy," she cooed. "It's hard to hit me when I'm walking, isn't it?"

Rick was going to hop down to lead her to the sound, but when he stopped to listen, the sound had stopped. "OK Jamie," said Sue, "let's have the baby cry again."

Sue was walking again when Rick heard the crying. He trotted behind her, waiting for the moment to jump. As she slowed to turn back the other way, Rick jumped up lightly against her. "Good Boy! How quickly you learn things," said Sue while feeding him a little square treat. "OK, where is the sound?"

As soon as he had finished the treat, Rick jumped down and trotted into the other room. He sat at the crib as Sue approached. Sue gave him a few pats and then reached into her pocket and dramatically pulled out a tug-of-war.

"Hey, Look what I have here," said Sue. "Would you like to have this?" She held the rag out to Rick and then pulled it back. She dangled it above his head, dropping it down to his level, and then jerking it up high again. Rick was bouncing up and down trying to reach the rag. Sue lowered it again, and Rick grabbed it. He pulled against Sue for a moment until she let go. He raced in and out of the room triumphantly waving the cloth for all to see.

Jamie came out from behind the desk and tried to grab the trailing end. Rick saw him and quickly changed direction. What fun he was having! Jamie laughed and said, "You're too fast for me, Rick." Sue smiled at Jamie's futile attempts to take the rag.

Soon all three were playing a fast-paced game of tug-of-war. Jamie and Sue each had the rag for a short time, but they quickly let Rick take it from them. Rick was thrilled. This was fun and exciting! It was as much fun to play with these trainers as with the other dogs, and they didn't mind when he took the rag from them. In fact, they seemed very pleased each time he pulled the cloth away.

Rick was sorry when the game finally ended and Sue took him back to his cage. He had really enjoyed his training that day. It was a fun challenge to try to hit a moving target when he heard a sound, and playing with the knotted cloth afterwards was great!

Chapter 8
The Mall

Rick was excited! Where were they going? Sue had put him and Maggsy in the back of the van after giving each of them a bath that morning. Rick had watched Maggsy submit to the water treatment, and had been only slightly offended when Sue washed him. After they were dry, Sue had buckled new, stiff orange collars around each of their necks.

Rick hoped that Sue was taking them back to her house. That was the only place he had been driven since he came to the training center, and he liked it there. Maybe he'd get to see Todd and play with Annie again.

They drove for what seemed to Rick a long time. Finally the van stopped and Sue opened the back door. The dogs had been taught not to jump out unless told to, so they kept back from the door and waited to see what Sue was going to do. Sue fastened an orange vest around Maggsy and then clipped a leash to her collar.

"OK Maggsy," said Sue. Maggsy jumped to the ground and bounced up and down. Maggsy was normally a happy dog, and right now she was happy and excited. She looked like a puffy cloud with her soft, curly clean white hair. Sue told Rick she'd be back soon, gave him a pat on the head and then closed the door.

Rick wished that he could have gone with Sue too. He didn't want to stay in the van by himself while Maggsy got to go have fun. Rick found that by standing on his hind legs he could just see out of the window in the back door. He saw Sue and Maggsy walking across the parking lot and then watched as the trainer and dog entered a huge, light-colored building. Rick's hind legs were getting tired and there was nothing else to look at except rows of parked cars, so he brought his front paws back to the floor.

Rick lay down and looked around the van. The back part of the van, the part he was in, was separated from the front by a metal screen. There were a few empty cages in the back with him. He nosed the doors open and checked to see if there was any food left in them. Nope; they were very empty.

As Rick lay down again, he saw a tiny shape wedged between the screen and one of the cages. He reached in with a paw and tried to drag it out. He could barely reach it. After a few tries he pulled the little thing out. It was a soft, rubberish pig. Rick licked it. It tasted like dog food. Rick nibbled on its tiny little head. *Oink*, it said. Rick poked it with a paw. *Oooiink!* came the sound again. Rick liked the taste of the little pig and enjoyed chewing on the soft, round head. It was very relaxing . . . Soon Rick dropped off to sleep.

Clank! came the sound of a key turning in the back door of the van. Rick jumped up. He looked attentively at the door. Sue must be back!

Sue opened the door, patted the floor of the van and said, "Jump up here, Maggsy." Maggsy jumped in. Now it was Rick's turn to have the vest put on him. Then Sue fastened on the leash and they were off.

Rick was full of energy and trotted ahead of Sue. He felt a sudden tug on the leash and remembered that he should be heeling. Rick slowed his pace and kept one eye on Sue's left leg so he could stay exactly even with her. Sue stopped. Rick was ready for that and quickly sat down. He had been taught to sit whenever he was heeling next to Sue and she stopped.

Sue said "Good Boy, Rick," and gave him a pat on the head. As Sue began walking again, Rick stood up and kept pace with her. Rick was very proud of how well he was doing and pranced in high steps next to his trainer.

Sue stopped at the wide, glass entrance doors that led into the building. Rick again sat. "Stay," Sue commanded as she stepped a few feet away from him. She walked in a circle around Rick, being careful to lift the leash over his head as she went around. Rick sat glued to the spot, but turned his head to follow Sue. "Good Boy!" Sue exclaimed. "What a good dog you are." Sue was beside Rick again and scratched him behind the ears. "Now, remember to pay attention to me when we get inside."

Sue opened one of the doors, and they walked into the mall. As they walked down the center of a wide hallway, Rick tried to keep one eye on Sue and still take in all the things that were going on around him. A little girl was walking in front of them holding on to her mother's hand with one hand and an ice cream cone with the other. Rick could smell the ice cream and was staring at it when he felt a strong pull to the right. Sue had turned down another hallway. Sue gave him another tug as he hurried to catch up. When he was finally back at her side she reached down and petted him.

Sue was now having Rick do some obedience drills. He was told to heel, then she stopped and he sat, then she told him to lie down and to stay. Rick discovered that Sue had a pocket full of treats. Every few commands he would get one. Rick lost interest in his surroundings and kept his attention on Sue.

After lying down, sitting, staying, heeling, and sitting once more, Sue led Rick over to a bench. Sue sat down and told Rick that he could relax for a few minutes and look around. Rick had not been given any commands, so he decided to lie down.

Rick watched all the people walking by. Some people were carrying packages, others were pushing children in strollers, a few walked in pairs holding hands, and many people were holding things that smelled very good. One little boy dropped a twisted brown thing in front of him. As Rick inched toward it, he heard Sue say, "No!"

Rick learned that he couldn't eat anything on the floor. Sue dropped some treats in front of him and told him, "Leave it" before he had a chance to even think about eating them. Then she picked them up and handed them to him one by one saying, "OK." After a few repetitions of this, he figured out that he could only eat what Sue gave him, not things he found.

An older man came and sat down on the bench a little distance from Sue. "Why did you bring your dog in here?" he asked.

Sue answered, "This is a hearing dog in training." After taking in the man's surprised expression, Sue added, "Hearing dogs are guide dogs for deaf people and are allowed in all public places."

"I didn't know that there were guide dogs for the deaf," said the man.

"Hearing dogs aren't as common as some other service dogs," said Sue. "You can tell Rick is a hearing dog because of his orange collar and vest."

"Oh, yes," said the man while turning his head to read the printing on Rick's vest. "I can see that his vest says 'Hearing Dog'. What kind of a dog is Rick?"

Sue motioned for Rick to come over toward the man. "He's an Australian Shepherd mix," said Sue.

The man reached his hand toward Rick and asked, "Can I pet him? He certainly looks like an intelligent dog."

Sue answered, "Thanks for asking first. Yes, this is his first time to come to the mall and he'd love some attention." Rick was happily leaning against the man's legs and enjoying a good petting. Rick decided he liked coming to town and being fed treats, and being petted by nice people.

"How can Rick help a deaf person?" the man asked. "Does he pull the person to the doorbell or something?"

Sue explained that hearing dogs touch the deaf person with a paw when they hear a sound and then go sit next to the sound.

"Hmm, that would take quite a dog to learn all that," replied the man. "I guess Rick is an intelligent dog."

"Yeah," agreed Sue, "he's a pretty good boy." She reached down to pet Rick and then stood up. "Well, Rick and I have some more work to do. It was nice talking to you."

"Thanks for filling me in about hearing dogs," said the man. "It certainly is good work you're doing."

Sue smiled and thanked him, as she and Rick headed out into the stream of people. Rick and Sue walked up and down the long hallways. Every few minutes, Sue would stop to look at something in a store window and Rick would sit down next to her.

Sue and Rick then walked through a wide glass doorway into one of the stores. Rick was careful to stay very close to Sue because the aisles were narrow and crowded with people. When clothes on racks hung out over their path, Rick would duck and walk under the hanging things. Sue looked down and smiled as she saw Rick emerge from under a rack of girls' dresses.

They made a turn to the left and then stopped by a rack of funny round-shaped things. Sue put several in turn on her head and studied herself in a mirror. "Do you like this hat?" Sue asked Rick. Rick thought Sue looked silly with the big brown hat with the wide brim on her head. "I think I'll buy it for Todd," she said as she led Rick up to a counter.

The woman at the counter took Sue's money and put the hat into a bag. It wasn't until they were walking away that the woman saw Rick. "Oh! It's a dog," she exclaimed. "You can't bring dogs in here!"

Sue and Rick walked back to the counter, and Sue told the salesclerk that Rick was a hearing dog and was allowed in the mall. "Oh, I'm sorry," said the woman. "I didn't know about hearing dogs. Are there many living around here?"

Sue replied, "There are a few local deaf people with dogs, but most of the hearing dogs you'll see here are the ones we're training. We often bring them to the mall because it's a good place to teach them how to act in public."

The woman looked down at Rick, who was sitting at Sue's side, and said, "Well, he certainly is well behaved. How can I tell if a dog's a hearing dog? Don't they wear a harness or something?"

"Guide dogs for the blind wear a harness," explained Sue. "The way to recognize a hearing dog is to just look for the bright orange vest."

Sue and Rick left with their package and began walking back to the mall entrance. On their way they met several groups of children. A tall woman who was herding one group asked if the kids could pet Rick. The little ones began to swarm around Rick even as Sue said, "OK, just be careful not to pat him too hard and be careful around his eyes."

Rick was soon engulfed in five-and six-year-olds, and was loving every minute of it. Several hands stroked his back, and many more patted his head.

"What a nice dog."

"How soft he is . . ."

"What's your name?" came a young voice.

Sue answered, "His name is Rick and he is a guide dog for the deaf. See his bright orange vest? That shows you he's a special dog that alerts deaf people to sounds."

"Oooh," said a little girl.

"Good Boy, Rick," said a small boy, who was patting Rick's head.

The tall woman collected her charges and thanked Sue for letting them pet Rick. A tired Sue and Rick then left the mall and walked back to the van.

Chapter 9
A Decision is Made

Kathy was sitting behind the desk today and Rick could tell that she was getting frustrated. "Why won't you play with anything but the tug-of-war?" she asked. "Why not anything else?" A collection of plastic carrots, hamburgers, shoes, and ducks lay around Rick's feet, along with a hard rubber ball and a tennis ball.

"I give up, Sue," said Kathy. "He just doesn't go for any of these." Kathy turned to Rick and said, "OK Rick, why don't you pick out your own toy?" With that she completely pulled out the desk drawer she had been getting the toys from and dumped it onto the floor. Balls rolled and the squeaky toys *squeaked* as they landed in front of Rick.

Rick was surprised at the sudden appearance of so many things. He sniffed through them and grabbed the end of an old tug-of-war and trotted smartly over to Sue. Sue half-heartedly held the end of it as Rick made a big show of pulling it free.

"I guess he's just a one toy dog," said Sue resignedly. "It certainly wouldn't be an exciting reward for long, since he'd get to play with it every time he works any of the sounds." Sue and Kathy looked quietly at Rick.

Meanwhile, Rick decided that since no one would try to take the rag from him, he'd see what else was in that pile of toys. He nosed a piece of rawhide bone that smelled good, and then Rick saw the little pig he had chewed on in the van. He snapped up the pig and trotted away, *Oinking* as he went.

"Hey! What does he have?" asked Sue, jumping to her feet. Before Kathy could answer, Sue was next to Rick looking in his mouth. "Why, it's the little pig!" exclaimed Sue.

"I found it in the van the other day," said Kathy. "Gee, I wonder why he likes that toy and not any of the others?"

Rick didn't know what all the fuss was about, but he dropped the pig when Sue reached for it. "Do ya like this little toy, Rick?" asked Sue, holding it out to him. Rick carefully picked up the pig off of Sue's hand and began chewing on its head.

"He really likes it!" squealed Sue. She took it from Rick again and tossed it down the room. Rick raced to where it landed, picked it up and carried it back to Sue. "What a wonderful boy!" sang Sue while giving Rick a hug.

Rick was glad Sue was so happy, but he wasn't quite sure why. He settled down on the rug near Sue's chair and gnawed softly on the pig's little, round head.

Kathy said, "I wrote 'plays with pink pig' in his

training notes. Who would've thought that he'd like the pig and not any of the other squeaky toys?"

"Maybe it's because the pig is such soft rubber," said Sue. "I hadn't really noticed, but we do seem to be out of the softer squeaky toys. Willy, that little dachshund Jane trained, destroyed most of them before he left.

"It could be that he likes it because it's so tiny," stated Kathy. "Remember that schnauzer I had a while ago? He'd only play with the pig and those little squeaky mice we used to have." Rick chewed contentedly on the pig while Kathy and Sue discussed his fate.

Rick was sitting beside Sue in the office. He had been here briefly a few times before, but today they were certainly staying a long time. Rick looked around at the tall cabinets, the desks, and the people moving in businesslike fashion around the room. Usually, when he and Sue came in, at least some of the people would talk to him or give him a pat, but today everyone looked busy.

Sue was sitting in a chair talking to someone behind a desk. It wasn't one of the trainers but an older man with white hair and a gray mustache. The man said, "I've called the Heralds, and they said any week next month would be fine."

"OK George, why don't we make it August 20th through 26th?" Sue suggested, looking at George's calendar. "I think Rick will need at least three more weeks before he's ready to go."

"All right," George answered, "I'll make the plane and hotel reservations this afternoon."

"By the way," said Sue, "what did Mr. Herald sound like on the phone? Was he excited about finally getting a dog for his wife?"

"Well," George began, "I think so. He seemed interested in the dog and concerned about his wife, Cynthia, who stays at home alone during the day. Until this year he worked at home for a computer software company, but now he has been promoted and has to go into the office every day."

"So now he worries about his wife being alone during the day?" Sue interrupted.

"Correct," answered George. "He said he will feel better about going to work when his wife has her hearing dog."

"Didn't she say something in her application about taking care of grandchildren?" asked Sue.

"Yes, he mentioned that to me today. Apparently, their daughter and her husband both work, so most days Cynthia takes care of the three children," explained George.

"Well, that sounds great," said Sue. "Rick really likes kids. I think this will be the perfect family for him."

"Come on, Rick," Sue said, getting to her feet. "We've got a lot left to teach you before we send you to be Cynthia's new ears."

Chapter 10
Rick Goes to Dallas

Rick looked around at all the people sitting and standing in the large area with huge glass windows on both sides. He wondered where they were and why they were here. Rick heard loud noises coming from outside and looked out the dark windows, trying to see what was happening.

Sue had taken Rick home the night before, but instead of playing and practicing sounds they had gone to bed early. They had gotten up early that morning too. Rick remembered how dark it had been when Sue let him and Annie out into the fenced back yard.

Soon after they had come back into the house, there had been a knock at the door. Although sleepy, Rick had run to touch Sue and then went and sat at the door.

It was Todd! Rick had been happy to see Todd, and Todd seemed happy to see him, too. Todd had then driven all of them in his pickup truck to this large, noisy place. Todd had put Rick and Annie in the back of the truck, and then he and Sue had climbed in front.

Rick had never been in a truck before and had been a little nervous. The truck was like the van, but the floor was just cold metal except for a rug where both dogs had stood. There were also windows all the way around, so it had been easy to see outside. Annie had seemed to like riding in the truck; she stared out the back window and every once in a while found something to bark at. Soon Rick had relaxed too, and stood next to the other dog watching the dark scenery blur by.

After a short drive, the truck had stopped and Sue had put on his vest and leash and then walked him up to this building. Todd had followed carrying a big suitcase. They had waited in line at a long desk and then walked to this area with all the people and chairs.

"We will begin general boarding for flight #308 for Dallas momentarily," said a voice from nowhere. "At this time we will board those passengers traveling with children and those that need a few extra minutes to board the plane."

"Well, that's us," said Sue, rising to her feet. "Take good care of Annie while I'm gone," she said to Todd.

Todd was now standing, too; he gave Sue a hug and a kiss. "You take care of yourself and Rick, and watch out for the traffic in Dallas." As Todd let her go, he said, "I'll see you on Sunday."

Sue and Rick hurried to where a young man was standing next to an open door. Sue handed him some papers and waited while he looked down disapprovingly at Rick.

"I'm sorry," the man said. "All pets must be in cages and checked at the counter."

"This is a hearing dog," explained Sue. "He has permission to come on the flight; see, they've written that on my ticket . . . Here is his ID card," Sue said while fumbling with her envelope of papers.

"Oh yes, I'm sorry," apologized the man as he looked at the card Sue handed him. "You can go right ahead."

Sue turned to wave at Todd and then walked with Rick down a long enclosed passageway and onto the plane. A smiling woman showed them to their seat in the front row. Sue had Rick sit down between the wall and her legs. "This will be fun, Rick. You just relax for a few hours and we'll get you to your new home."

Rick watched as many other people walked past their row of seats. Suddenly, a young woman holding a little girl by the hand swung into their row and sat down.

"Oh, look at the puppy!" squealed the girl.

"What is a dog doing on the plane?" asked the woman in an unfriendly tone.

Sue explained that Rick was a hearing ear dog on his way to meet his new deaf mistress.

"Oh," came the woman's icy reply. "Well, please keep him away from me. I don't like dogs."

There were three seats in their row with Sue closest to the window. The little girl sat next to Sue and her mother sat next to the aisle. The woman kept looking over at Rick disapprovingly and told the girl not to pay any attention to him.

Soon the airplane began to move. It moved faster and faster and then tilted sharply upwards. Rick could hear the sound of muffled engines. He looked up at Sue, but since she didn't look worried, he decided it was okay. He sat quietly between Sue and the plane wall, while Sue softly stroked his head.

Despite her mother's warnings, the little girl sneaked her hand over Sue's knees and patted Rick. Rick leaned against Sue to make it easier for the girl to reach him. Eventually the woman glanced at them. She looked like she was going to say something, but then seemed to change her mind. Finally she spoke to Sue, "He really is well behaved, isn't he? I guess he wouldn't be allowed on the plane unless he was well trained."

Sue explained the training process and then agreed saying, "Yes, by the time they get this far, they are very well behaved."

"Where is he going?" asked the woman.

"Rick here," said Sue as she gave his head a pat, "is going to a deaf woman in Dallas. She's alone during the day taking care of her grandchildren and needs to be able to hear sounds like the doorbell, smoke alarm, or one of the children calling for her."

The woman looked at Rick again and said, "What a wonderful thing for a dog to be able to do." She leaned back into her seat and smiled. Eventually the child stopped petting him, and Rick lay down.

A few hours later Rick suddenly felt the floor drop out from under him and heard a whining sound from the engines. Rick sat up and looked worriedly at Sue. Sue reached down and patted him. "It's OK, Rick. The plane is just coming down to land. We'll be on the ground again soon."

Rick felt reassured by Sue's quiet voice, but didn't like the loud noise and the feeling of falling. *Bump! Bump!* Rick heard a muffled noise and felt the floor lurch beneath him. He sat very still and leaned against Sue's legs . . . and then it was all over. People began standing up and moving around. Sue patted Rick and said, "Come on, we're here."

As they stood up and began to leave, the woman who had been sitting next to them said to a man behind her, who was looking down at Rick, "He's a hearing ear dog and is going to help a deaf woman in Dallas. Isn't he a pretty dog?"

Rick and Sue walked off the plane and down long hallways full of people. Sue stopped at a counter, and then they walked over to a revolving belt that carried suitcases around and around. Rick watched as Sue grabbed the big case that Todd had carried into the airport earlier that day. "Let's go find our car, Rick," Sue said, as she tried to hold his leash and a small bag in one hand and the heavy suitcase in the other.

After Rick had drunk some water and had been walked in a grassy area, they drove off in a little light-colored car. Rick sat in the back seat, tilting his face up to catch the breeze from the partly opened window. They drove for a long time, stopping and starting often. Finally, Sue stopped in front of a brick house. "This is it," Sue said. "Take a look at your new home."

Chapter 11
Cynthia

Rick looked out the car window. He saw a two-story brick house that had several neatly trimmed shrubs in the front yard. He also saw a fence running behind the house, enclosing a big, grassy back lawn. Sue opened his door, snapped on his leash and said, "OK." Rick jumped lightly to the ground and followed Sue up to the front porch. Sue made a bell ring several times, but the door didn't open. After knocking with no response, Sue walked Rick over to the front window.

Rick watched in surprise as Sue jumped up and down and waved her arms. "There she is; she sees us now," said a breathless Sue. As they walked back to the front porch, the door opened and a middle-aged woman wearing a checked dress stood looking out at them.

"You must be Sue, and this must be my hearing dog," said the woman. "Sorry you had to wait. I wasn't in the living room where the doorbell light is," she apologized. Rick noticed something different about the woman's voice. She didn't speak the way anyone else he had heard did.

Sue began moving her hands and fingers in rapid motions. Rick noticed that the woman was watching the fingers and seemed to understand what was going on, because every once in a while she nodded. Sue moved her fingers again, but this time the woman just looked at her questioningly.

Sue said, "I can sign better if I talk too." She stood still with her eyebrows pulled together in concentration, and then began moving her hands again while saying slowly, "I often have trouble letting our new clients know when I've arrived. But, as soon as Rick starts working for you, it will be much easier."

This time the woman nodded, saying, "I've been looking forward to having help with sounds. Both of you, come on in."

Rick and Sue walked into the house and after sitting on a long couch, Sue unfastened Rick's leash. "What do you think of him, Cynthia?" Sue asked while signing.

"Oh . . . well, he's very unusual looking, don't you think?" said Cynthia. "But I can tell he's part collie."

"We think he's half collie and half Australian Shepherd," said Sue. "His coloring is Aussie, but he has the long collie hair."

Rick, now free, began to wander around the house. He sniffed his way around the living room and back into the dining room. He decided not to go too far from Sue, though, so he returned to the living room.

"Why don't we show Rick where the sounds are in your house? Then I'll leave the two of you to get acquainted," suggested Sue. "He's had a pretty tiring day flying, so he'll probably want to just nap and start getting used to his new home. Sue stood up and then signed and said to Cynthia, "But first let's see the rest of the house."

Sue and Cynthia began walking around the house, and Rick decided he'd better follow. In the kitchen Sue asked Cynthia to set off the oven timer and then to watch how Rick alerted her to the sound.

Buzzzzz! Buzzzz! Buzzzzz! Rick stopped and listened, and then jumped up and lightly touched Sue's legs. "Good Boy," said Sue. "Where's the sound?" Rick decided the sound was coming from the stove and hurried to sit next to it. "What a good boy!" exclaimed Sue. "Here Rick, go get the pig." Sue then tossed the little pig a short distance and watched as he pounced on it.

"Oh, my!" exclaimed Cynthia. "He really does tell you when there's a sound."

"He works all sounds about the same way," said Sue. "He taps you with a paw when he hears a sound and then leads you to it. You must make sure though, to always praise him when he taps you and especially when he gets to the sound."

"You mean pet him or give him a toy?" asked Cynthia.

"A pat on the head, or saying 'Good Boy' is about all you'll have time for when he touches you," said Sue. "Just make sure you give him lots more attention after he has sat down at the sound--like throwing a toy and playing with him."

Cynthia asked, "Will I have to keep toys in my pockets like you do?"

"It's probably easier to keep a toy he likes next to each sound. That way it's there when you need it," said Sue. "We'll go over all of this during the week; today we're just introducing the sounds."

"OK? Now what other sounds will you want him to work?" Sue asked. Cynthia led them upstairs and into a bedroom.

"We set the alarm every morning for Thomas to wake up to," Cynthia said. "Should Rick work that?"

"Does your husband hear the alarm and turn it off?" came Sue's question.

"Yes, he turns it off, and then wakes me up," Cynthia answered.

Sue responded, "Well, unless you go back to sleep and set the alarm later for yourself, Rick doesn't need to work it. You see, the sounds we have your dog work should be ones that you need. If we teach Rick to work the alarm, your husband will have to wait while Rick wakes you up, instead of turning it off when he hears it.

Sue continued, "If Tom is gone very much on travel and you need to set the alarm for yourself, then we probably should have Rick work it.

"Oh, no," said Cynthia. "My husband is never gone overnight."

"OK, then Rick won't do the alarm clock. At first he may try to work it, but if you don't praise him when he taps you, and you don't follow him to the clock, he will learn that it's a sound that he doesn't need to work," Sue explained.

"How about the telephone and doorbell?" asked Cynthia. "He will need to work those, right?"

Sue answered, "Yes, those you'll need, along with the smoke alarm, and the name call. Let's see . . . do you have a dryer with a buzzer?"

"Yes, but it's way down in the basement. "I don't really need it, because I just watch the clock to know when the clothes are done."

"Well, it's a sound Rick could help you with," said Sue. "Let's go downstairs and see how loud that buzzer is. If Rick can hear it from, say, the living room, he should be able to help you with laundry."

Rick worked the dryer buzzer, then the smoke alarm in the hallway, and then the doorbell. He felt challenged to locate all these new sounds in a new place and was pleased at how happy Sue was with him. After working the telephone, Sue gave him the tug-of-war to play with. He pulled it away from Sue and, though surprised, tugged it away from the new woman who had grabbed the free end. Cynthia tried once more to get it from Rick and then sat back into her chair.

Sue stood up and then turned toward Cynthia. "You two are going to need some time alone to get to know each other, so I'm going to leave now," Sue said while her fingers and hands moved rapidly. "You should read the information about hearing dogs I brought you, and spend a lot of time with Rick." Sue paused, "He's a little tired from the trip and from being in a new place, but see if he wants to play and later on you can feed him his dinner."

"Should I have my grandchildren over to meet him?" asked Cynthia.

"No," Sue quickly answered. "Rick needs to get to know you first. It's going to take awhile before he learns that he now has to work sounds for you. The more time he spends alone with you, the easier it will be for him. Maybe they can come over for a few minutes tomorrow."

As Sue headed for the door she turned and said, "I'll be back this evening to meet your husband and explain how he can help you and Rick get started."

Rick jumped to his feet when he saw Sue opening the door and ran over to her. "You stay here, Rick," said Sue. "I'll be back soon."

Sue was gone and Rick sat looking nervously at the door. Cynthia walked back to her chair and sat down. "Here Rick," she said. "Come over here with me." Rick looked at her and then slowly walked over. "It's all right, Rick. We're going to have a good time together and be good friends." She scratched him behind the ears, but he sat stiffly not really enjoying the attention.

"You are going to be my ears and help me take care of my grandchildren," Cynthia continued. "You'll like Billy and Tracy and little Joey, and I just know they will like you." She seemed to notice Rick's strained expression, and reached down with both hands to pet him. "You're going to be just fine, honey. I know you'll miss being with Sue, but you're going to like your new home here."

Rick was lying in the living room at Cynthia's feet when the doorbell rang. He jumped to his feet and then looked worriedly around. "What is it, Rick?" asked Cynthia looking up. "Oh! The doorbell light is flashing. You must hear the bell." She stood up and walked to the door with Rick nervously pacing in circles behind her.

"Thomas," Cynthia said in a surprised tone, "Why did you ring the bell?"

"Hi, Honey," said Mr. Herald while moving his fingers and gesturing with his hands. "I thought I'd give Rick a chance to work. He's here, isn't he?"

"Yes, he and Sue came this afternoon," said Mrs. Herald while closing the door behind her husband, "but we're not supposed to practice sounds yet."

"Let's see this guy," said Thomas walking around his wife toward Rick. "Hey there, Rick; come and say hello." Thomas reached down and patted Rick. Rick thought this new man was very friendly, like Todd. He leaned against Thomas' legs and enjoyed the attention.

Rick ate his dinner out of his new metal dog dish while Thomas and Cynthia ate their dinner at the table. Afterwards they were all getting settled in the living room when the doorbell rang. *Flash, Flash* went the little red light mounted on the wall, *Bing, Bong,* came the sound from the doorbell.

Rick looked at the light and cocked his head to hear the sound better as he tried to figure out what he was supposed to do. Mr. Thomas had risen from his chair when the bell began and now opened the door for Sue. When Rick saw who was there, he let out a joyous bark and ran to greet his trainer.

"Hey there, Rick," Sue laughed, "I've only been gone a few hours." She shook Thomas' outstretched hand and greeted him too. "How are you all getting along?" Sue asked Thomas while moving her fingers for Cynthia to see.

"He seems to be settling down a little," answered Cynthia. "He was upset after you left, but he did lie down and take a nap before Thomas came home."

"He's quite a dog," announced Thomas. "I think he's going to be a great help. He jumped right up when you rang the doorbell."

"Good Boy," said Sue to Rick. Rick watched her walk across the room and then sit in a soft-looking chair. He trotted over and sat very close to her feet.

Cynthia and Thomas sat back in their places on the couch and looked at Sue and Rick. "He seems awfully attached to you," Cynthia said. "I hope he'll like me as much."

"Oh, he will, Cynthia," Sue said reassuringly. "By the end of the week he'll have learned to take you to the sounds instead of me, and after I've gone, you two will grow closer and closer."

Sue turned to Thomas, "It will be hard for you, because I can tell you like dogs, but for the first few weeks your job will be to ignore Rick as much as possible. Cynthia needs to be the one who feeds him, plays with him, and takes him outside."

"I'll do my best," he replied. "What else can I do to help them?"

"Starting tomorrow, when we have taught Rick to go to Cynthia when he hears sounds, you can help them practice."

"You mean ring the doorbell and things?" Thomas asked.

"Yeah," agreed Sue. "Every day when you come home from work, you can ring the bell instead of coming in. If Cynthia tells you that Rick was slow or something, then you can ring it a few more times."

"What about the name call?" asked Cynthia.

"Thomas will need to practice that with you too," Sue answered, "as well as the smoke alarm." She added, "The smoke alarm hopefully won't go off too often on its own, so you should practice it several times a week at first, and then when Rick is working it well, once or twice a month."

A short time later Sue left again and, though Rick tried to stay awake in case she came back, he finally drifted off to sleep next to Thomas and Cynthia's bed. His new, soft dog bed was so comfortable . . .

Chapter 12
Training with Cynthia

During the next few days, Rick got used to his new schedule. Every morning Sue would come and they would practice sounds for a while. After Sue left, Cynthia would take him for a walk or put him outside in the fenced back yard. Then Sue would come back and they would practice sounds again.

Rick was a little confused, though, when they were practicing. Sue didn't seem to want him to tap her anymore when he heard a sound, but seemed pleased when he touched Cynthia instead. He had learned that Cynthia kept little treats in her pockets. She gave him one most of the time when he touched her with a paw. She was also the one who would play with him now at the door, stove, smoke alarm and telephone.

Sometimes he practiced sounds with Cynthia when Sue wasn't there. He had taken her to the door several times and had found Thomas waiting there. Thomas would give them both a hug as he came in. Rick liked that.

Yesterday, Rick had met Billy, Tracy, and Joey. They had each wanted to pet him and throw the pig for him to chase. The kids were here today, too, in the living room playing with his toys. Rick watched them with interest for awhile, but soon realized that they were just going to play with each other and not toss anything for him to chase. Rick sighed and rested his head on his paws.

Rrrrrr! Rrrrrr! Rrrrrr! came a loud sound from upstairs. Rick jumped up. Where was Cynthia? He found her standing in the kitchen looking out the window. After lightly jumping up against her, he galloped back through the living room and dashed up the stairs. Cynthia followed at a slower pace and patted him on the head as he sat under the smoke alarm.

Rick saw Sue, who was standing on a chair underneath the smoke detector, gesturing to Cynthia. "You need to reward him," Sue said out loud. "Try to remember to keep a toy in your pocket or keep one near this sound." With that Sue reached into her pocket and tossed a knotted rag over his head. Cynthia caught it and held it just out of Rick's reach. Rick jumped up and snatched it out of her hand.

"That's the way," Sue said. "We need to make it really exciting for him when he gets you to a sound. A pat on the head is OK, but especially now while he's learning to work for you, we want him to get a big reward."

"Grab the rag away from him and throw it down the hall," Sue suggested. Rick let Cynthia take the cloth from him and then raced down the hallway after it as she gave it a toss.

"Will I always have to play with him so much at the sounds?" Cynthia asked. "What about when people come to the door? I can't very well make them wait outside while I play with Rick, can I?"

"I'm sure your friends will be glad to cooperate," said Sue. "And when Rick has things all figured out, you won't have to make such a big deal about each sound. But he will always need some praise."

Sue sat down on the folding chair that she had been standing on. "Cynthia, I know it seems hard to remember everything right now, but don't worry; eventually it will all be second nature. In a few weeks it will seem very natural to tell Rick 'Good Boy' at sounds and then get him started playing with a toy. Then you can greet people at the door or on the phone, or take care of food in the oven."

"I didn't realize how much work it would be to get started with a dog," said Cynthia. "I just hope everything works out as easily as you think it will."

"Grandma! Grandma!" came a shout from downstairs.

Rick turned his head to hear the sound and noticed that Sue did too, but that Cynthia was not responding. Rick was starting to sort this out when Sue sprang up and headed down the stairs. Rick and Cynthia followed her down into the living room.

"What's going on down here?" Sue asked the children.

Billy looked up with a red face as Tracy pointed an accusing finger at him and said, "Billy won't give my doll back."

"Well, she took the pig away from me," Billy whined.

Cynthia seemed to understand what had happened and took the doll from Billy and gave it back to Tracy.

Sue studied the scene and said while signing, "Cynthia, they seem to think that Rick's toys are things that they can play with too. They need to know that they must leave Rick's things alone, and Rick will learn that he can't play with their toys either."

Cynthia reached for Rick's toy pig that Tracy was holding tightly in one hand.

"No, No!" screamed Tracy. "This is my toy!"

"Tracy, you must let go of the pig," Cynthia said quietly. "That is Rick's toy and you mustn't play with it. Why don't you play with your dolly?"

Tracy finally loosened her grip on the pig, but instead of giving it to her grandmother she hurled it at Rick.

Thump, the pig bounced off Rick's side. Rick reacted quickly and ran to hide under the table.

"OK kids, listen up," said Sue in a commanding voice. Billy, Tracy and even little Joey looked up at her. Sue sat down on the floor next to them and began, "I know you realize that your grandmother can't hear very well."

"She's deaf," piped up Tracy.

"Yes, that's right," said Sue, "and she wants Rick to help her know when there are sounds. Rick has a hard job to do. He has to always be listening so he can tell Grandma when someone is at the door, or calling on the phone, or when one of you needs her help." Sue paused and watched the young faces.

Rick heard Sue say his name several times, so he came out from under the table and lay down next to her. As she reached down to pet him she began talking again. "Rick won't be able to help your grandmother if you are bothering him. You must not take his toys, you must never throw things at him, and you must not chase him around. He is Grandma's dog and you must leave him alone. Do you understand?"

Billy asked, "Well, we can play with him can't we?"

"You can play with him outside in the backyard when Grandma says you can, but in the house you need to leave him alone," Sue answered.

Sue then turned to Cynthia who was now sitting on the couch, "I have been telling them that they must leave Rick alone in the house." Sue was using her fingers and hands like she usually did when talking to the children's grandmother, but this time her gestures were much bigger than normal.

"I have told them that too," said Cynthia, "but they don't seem to want to listen to me. I talked to Kris and Bob about it, too, last evening when they came for the kids."

"I guess you'll just have to watch them closely for the next few weeks and make sure that they learn from the start that there are rules about Rick," said Sue. "It's natural for them to want to play with Rick and then be mad or jealous when they can't."

"I'll make sure that they behave themselves," Cynthia promised as she picked up the squeaky pig from the floor and put it into her pocket.

Sue stood up and said, "Let's have the kids practice doing the name call with us. That will get them involved and should help them understand what this is all about."

"Children," said Cynthia, "we are going to practice the name call with Rick. Billy, you will be first, all right?"

"What am I 'posed to do?" asked Billy.

"Rick is going to learn to go and get your grandma when you call her name," explained Sue. "Why don't you sit in that chair," she pointed, "and call out Grandma, Grandma, all right?"

"OK," said Billy. He climbed up in the chair and then shouted "Grandma! Grandma! Grandmaaa!"

Rick looked over at him. What a strange sound Billy was making! Rick looked up at Sue, but Sue looked away. Then Rick remembered that he was supposed to get Cynthia. He trotted over to her and received a yummy treat as soon as his front paw touched her leg.

"Good Boy," said Cynthia. "What is it?"

"Keep yelling," Sue said to Billy.

"Grandma! Grandma!" cried Billy.

Rick sat down next to Billy's chair and looked back at Sue to see if she was pleased. "Here Rick," said Cynthia, "go get your pig." She tossed his pig a few feet. Rick immediately pounced on the little pig.

Sue turned to Billy. "That was very good, Billy. When you need your grandmother, call her name out loudly like you just did and wait for Rick to bring her to you."

Billy smiled at the praise and reached down to pet Rick who had retrieved his pig.

"It's OK to pet him when he brings Grandma," said Sue. "That will let him know that he did a good job."

"And, Cynthia, that was perfect!" Sue said excitedly using big hand movements. "You had his toy ready and everything."

"My turn! My turn!" screamed Tracy.

"OK," said Sue, "You can take your brother's place in the chair and do just what he did."

Rick had a busy afternoon leading Cynthia from the dining room, kitchen, basement, and upstairs bedroom to one of the calling children. Finally, Sue said that was enough for the day.

"We will practice name calls tomorrow too," Sue promised the kids. "Isn't it fun to help Grandma train her dog?" Without waiting for an answer she went on, "If you are good tomorrow and don't take Rick's toys, we will also let you ring the door bell for us."

After Sue left, Rick curled up on his new cushion next to the sofa and promptly went to sleep.

Chapter 13
Rick on His Own

"Good morning, Dallas. This is KJKK bringing you all the morning news." The sudden voice startled Rick awake. Then realizing that the voice was the radio that came on every morning, he settled back down. He knew that Thomas would eventually turn off the sound and then get out of bed.

Rick followed Thomas downstairs and stood looking at the back door. "Do you want to go out, Rick?" asked Thomas as he opened the door. Rick trotted out into the early morning air and ran sniffing around the yard. Soon he saw the door open again, and he came back into the house.

Rick watched as Thomas ate his breakfast and realized that he was getting hungry too. Rick licked his empty dish and it banged into the wall with a metal "*Clang!*"

Thomas looked up. "Would you like your breakfast, Rick? Don't see why you should have to wait until Cynthia gets up. I'll feed you now." Thomas gave Rick an affectionate pat as he set down the full dish in front of him.

After finishing his meal, Rick wandered into the living room and lay down on his cushion. He watched as Thomas put on his coat and went out the front door.

Click, went the lock on the door, and Rick was alone. He lay sprawled across his cushion, thinking. He had gotten used to living with Thomas and Cynthia now, but he missed Sue. He had spent several mornings waiting for her to come again, but she had not returned.

Rick had been longing for a home and people, ever since his family had left him at the shelter. But now that he had both, he still wasn't quite happy. One thing that was bothering him was the sounds. He had learned to jump right up and take Sue to sounds that he heard and tried to do the same with Cynthia.

When Sue had been coming every day, Cynthia had been good at giving him treats and toys when he alerted her. But now, sometimes Cynthia wouldn't even go with him to the sounds. Yesterday when Rick heard the buzzer down in the basement, he had tapped her on the knee and then went to sit at the dryer. Rick waited for Cynthia to come down, but she hadn't followed. He ran up and down the stairs to get her, but she just wouldn't come with him. Finally, she had put him outside in the yard.

Rick was feeling very confused. He was used to getting played with and receiving a lot of attention when he worked well. Sue had always smiled and talked to him and would throw one of his toys, but Cynthia often ignored him after he took her to the doorbell or the oven. Sometimes Thomas would play with him, though, and that was fun.

Bing! Bong! came the ring from the front door. Rick looked up the stairs and decided to go find Cynthia. She was in the bedroom looking out a window. Rick tapped her with a paw and trotted down to sit at the door. Rick waited patiently as she opened the door for the three children, but she gave her attention to them, not to him. As the kids trooped into the house, Rick went back and lay on his cushion. Soon he was asleep.

Rick suddenly woke up. Ouch! Something was pulling on his tail! He lifted his head to see Tracy holding the end of his tail, ready to pull again.

"You're 'posed to leave Rick alone," said Billy. "I'm gonna go tell Grandma."

"He doesn't care," said Tracy. "See?"

"I can make him move," cried Billy. "Gi'me that ball," he said to Joey, grabbing the toy from his brother's tiny hands.

The ball hit Rick with a bump. He jumped up and hurried into the dining room.

"Hey, he wants to play!" shouted Tracy. "Let's chase him."

Tracy and Billy ran after Rick with Joey toddling along behind. Rick ran through the dining room and then into the kitchen. He ducked under the kitchen table and wormed through the chair legs until he was at a safe distance from the grabbing hands.

Rick was tired of the kids. It seemed like every time he tried to get Cynthia for a sound, one of them would hit him or pull his hair. Why didn't Cynthia make the children leave him alone, like Sue had?

After several weeks of abuse by the children, Rick had just about given up trying to alert Cynthia to sounds. One evening as he lay on his cushion, he heard the doorbell ring. He thought about getting Cynthia, but he knew she was sitting on the floor in the back bedroom with the kids. *Bing! Bong!* came the sound again. Rick looked up at Thomas who was sitting in the living room reading the paper. Rick laid a paw softly on Thomas' knee and then ran to sit at the door.

"Huh--oh, are you telling me someone's at the door, Rick? You should be telling Cynthia, but let's go see who's there." Before opening the door, Thomas tossed Rick the squeaky pig that was sitting on a shelf nearby. Rick pounced on the pig and then carried it back to his cushion.

Rick looked up as Thomas opened the door. Suddenly he heard a familiar voice! Rick dropped the pig and ran to the door. It was Jamie! Rick pushed his way between Thomas and the door and bounced up and down in front of Jamie.

"Hey, Rick. How'ya doing?" asked Jamie

"Well, Rick sure seems to know you," said Thomas. "Please, come in."

As the two got settled into chairs, Jamie asked, "Where's Cynthia?"

"Oh, she's back with the kids," replied Thomas. "I'll send Rick to get her." He turned to Rick and said, "OK boy, go get Grandma."

Rick started down the hallway to get Cynthia, but after seeing that she was still playing with the kids, he stopped. He decided to go lie down under the kitchen table instead.

"Rick," called Thomas. "Where's Cynthia?"

Rick lay where he was. He wanted to please Thomas, but he didn't want to be attacked again by the kids. Rick saw Jamie's feet approaching and then saw his face as he peered under the table.

"Hey, what's the matter Rick?" Jamie softly asked. "Come on out here."

Rick crept out and lay down next to Jamie. Jamie pet Rick gently and looked thoughtful. Finally, he stood up and went back into the living room. Rick slowly followed and lay down near Jamie's feet.

"Hey Thomas, what's going on here?" asked Jamie. "Why isn't Rick working? Why does he seem afraid to go to Cynthia?"

Thomas answered in a concerned tone, "I really don't know. Rick worked well the first few weeks, but now he's acting very strangely. He came and got me when you rang the doorbell. Actually . . . he's been coming to me more than Cynthia, at least when I'm home in the evenings."

"It might have something to do with the children," Thomas suggested. "He seems to hide under the table a lot when they are here."

"That's odd," said Jamie. "He's always seemed to like kids." Jamie looked down thoughtfully at Rick and said, "Well, I'm glad I stopped by. There seems to be a definite problem here. I came by just to see how you all were doing since I'm delivering another hearing dog nearby. Sue wanted me to be sure to check on you."

"I'm glad you've come." Thomas sounded relieved as he continued, "I had wanted Cynthia to write to the center in her next progress report and let you know that we've been having problems, but she seemed to think we could work this out ourselves."

"Why don't you tell me what you've noticed?" suggested Jamie, "then I'll go talk to Cynthia."

The next day Jamie was back and he, Cynthia, and the kids were all in the kitchen. Jamie signed to Cynthia as he spoke, "I need to make a phone call and then I'll let myself out. I can see you're really busy in here."

"Yes, go ahead," came Cynthia's reply. I'm going to give the children their lunch. Rick watched as Joey struggled to get out of his high chair while the two older kids were fighting over one of his toys.

Jamie walked into the living room and Rick followed. "Hello; Yes this is Jamie . . . I'd like to talk to Sue if she's available," Jamie said as he held the phone.

"Hey, Sue, sorry to give you some bad news, but there's a real problem here. Rick spends most of his time hiding under the table. He won't hit Cynthia anymore for sounds . . . No, he seems to be working Thomas instead."

"Some of it may be the grandchildren . . . I don't know . . . I was here last night too."

"OK, I'll talk to Cynthia and Thomas some more, but I think I better bring Rick back. He's not happy here and looks kind of thin, too . . . Yeah, I'll let you know."

Jamie began walking back toward the kitchen but then stopped and watched the scene from the doorway. Joey sat in a high chair banging his spoon on his plate, while Billy and Tracy fought loudly over who would get the last muffin. Cynthia had called Rick and set down his food dish, but instead of eating, Rick just lay on the floor and looked back and forth between Tracy and Billy. Finally, Rick took a bite of his food and then dashed into the living room to lie on his cushion.

Rick could hear Cynthia and Jamie talking in the kitchen, but he wasn't going back in there. The children's loud screams made him uneasy, so he was staying out here, away from the confusion and noise.

Chapter 14
Will Rick Get Washed Out?

Rick was again in a kennel at the training center. Sue had been happy to see him, and he was happy to be back. He quickly got back in the routine of playing outside with the dogs and taking Sue to sounds in the training apartment. He felt sad when he noticed that none of his friends were here anymore. Mickey, Maggsy, and the other dogs he knew best were all gone. He wondered if they had gone to live with people like he had.

"Rick, go and get Sue," called Jane from the other room. Rick jumped up and looked for Sue. She had just been sitting at the desk, but where was she now? Rick hurriedly searched the room. There she was under the desk! Rick tapped her and dashed back to sit next to Jane.

"Good Boy, Rick!" exclaimed Sue. "What do we have for such a good dog?"

"How about a mouse?" said Jane pulling a tiny mouse out of her pocket. *Squeak! Squeak!*

Rick kept his eyes on the squeaking mouse and zoomed after it the moment Jane tossed it. He liked the little mouse. It was soft like the pig. He carried it over to the rug, squeaking it as he went.

"He seems to be working good now," said Jane. "But he sure was a mess the first week."

"Yeah, he was awfully nervous," agreed Sue. "I wonder what went on at Cynthia's house."

"Jamie said he seemed afraid of the kids," replied Jane. "I can't really believe it, unless they were really wild."

"They weren't very well behaved," stated Sue, "but I thought Cynthia would be able to control them. It's funny; the interviewers who talked to them right after she applied for a dog said the grandchildren were just fine."

Jane responded, "Well, that interview was done more than a year ago, so the kids were all much younger."

"Yeah, that could be," agreed Sue. "What I can't understand is why Rick would start working Thomas instead of Cynthia. Thomas knew that he wasn't supposed to pay any attention to Rick, and he said that he hadn't." Sue was quiet for a minute and then went on, "I'm just wondering whether we should try placing Rick again."

"Everybody should be here tomorrow, so let's talk about it then," suggested Jane. "He seems OK now and it would really be a shame to have to wash out a dog that's working so well."

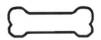

Rick was back in the little training building again and wondered why all of the trainers were suddenly so quiet. He looked at each of them-- Jane was sitting at the desk tapping her pen, Jamie was sitting in a chair near the desk, Kathy was at the kitchen table, and Sue was on the floor next to him, brushing his hair. Rick was glad to relax for awhile after practicing so many sounds, but he wondered what would happen next. All four trainers had been talking for the last few minutes and then had abruptly lapsed into silence.

"OK," said Sue, "Then where are we going to send him?"

Jane began looking through a stack of papers lying on the desk. As she thumbed through the stack, she said, "George brought over all the applications--but it looks like they're mostly for medium or small dogs." After a short pause she added, "Only three people want a large dog."

"Tell us about those then," said Kathy.

"Let's see . . . there's a Mr. Roberts, 36 years old with a wife and son in Missouri. He and his wife are both teachers. He teaches at a high school for the deaf, and umm . . . his wife teaches at the public high school."

"They sound very active too," said Jane continuing. "They bike-ride and jog, and the whole family goes camping and hiking on weekends."

"Hey, he sounds really good for Rick," said Jamie. "What kind of dogs has he had before?"

Jane answered. "He's had a whippet and a greyhound. Oh! Never mind . . . he says he wants a short haired dog because of his wife's allergies."

"Rick is definitely not short haired," said Sue, stretching a strand of his hair out to its full length. "And he should probably not go to a family that has children. Who else is there?"

"There's a Mrs. Scott in Southern Oregon," said Jane. "She's seventy-five years old . . . and lives by herself in the country. She's had a progressive hearing loss since age 50 and, yeah . . . seems to really love dogs."

"She sounds great," said Kathy, "but can she handle a large dog?"

"It says here," Jamie said while reading over Jane's shoulder, "that she raised and trained German Shepherds for years and is still quite active. This interview was done last year, though, so we should have the office check on her health and talk to her a little."

"Who's the third person?" asked Sue.

"It's that college girl in New York whose parents filled out the application," Jane reported.

"Oh, yeah," said Sue without enthusiasm, "I remember that one. Let's hope that Mrs. Scott will work out for Rick."

Chapter 15
School Demonstration

Rick was standing in the back of the van with a little dachshund named Susie. They were both clean and brushed and were wearing their orange collars and vests. Rick wondered where they were going. Maybe they would go to the big building with all the stores and people again.

Rick could see Kathy and Sue sitting in the front of the van. They looked very different today. Instead of wearing their usual dark coveralls, they were wearing regular clothes.

Soon the van stopped and Kathy opened the back door. Rick remembered just in time not to jump out. Susie had dashed for the open door and jumped, only to be told "No!" by Kathy, who caught her in mid-jump and put her back inside. Now both doors were open, but the dogs sat still, attentively watching their trainers. Sue and Kathy had attached leashes to the dogs' collars and were standing motionless watching the dogs. Finally, Rick and Susie were told "OK," and in unison the two dogs jumped to the ground.

Rick walked on the left beside Sue, being careful not to rush ahead. "You're going to do a demo for the school today, Rick," explained Sue. "I want to see how you'll be around all the kids. I'm hoping you're not going to be afraid of all children now."

Rick and Susie were told to sit and stay near the edge of a large raised wooden platform that was at the end of a very big, empty room. Sue and Kathy were busy moving chairs and a table around and finally seemed happy with how things were set up.

Rick sat still but turned his head and saw and heard many children suddenly entering the room. The children were coming in through large doors that were now open on both sides of the room. Each group of kids was led by an adult, and it became very loud with the sound of so many feet and the voices and laughter of the children. The kids followed the grown-ups in straggling lines and then sat down in rows on the floor. As the room began to fill up, Rick began to feel nervous.

"Let's go meet some of the kids, Rick," said Sue as she picked up his leash and walked down the short stairway toward the crowd of people. Rick hesitated but then slowly followed Sue.

"This is Rick," Sue said to a small group of young children sitting on one side of the room. "Would you like to pet him? He likes to be petted, but please be gentle."

As eager hands reached out to Rick, Rick braced himself against Sue's legs. He was prepared for the worst. He knew what kids could be like . . . Hey . . . This was nice! The hands softly patted him. No one pulled his tail or his ears. Rick relaxed a little and began to enjoy the attention. He looked up at Sue and wagged his tail.

"This isn't so bad, is it?" asked Sue with a smile.

After Rick and Sue climbed back up the stairs to the stage, Kathy and Sue talked to the audience. Then the two dogs took turns taking Kathy and Sue to a ringing phone and kitchen timer that were set off. Rick liked it when all the people clapped for him. This was fun!

Sue then handed his leash to Kathy, went down the stairs, and walked down the center aisle between the groups of children to the very back of the room. Kathy told the group, "We are now going to do a Name Call. This is how a deaf person's family can get the deaf person to come to them." Kathy paused and then asked the crowd, "If you were deaf and your mother called you to dinner, you wouldn't be able to hear her, would you?"

A chorus of "No's" filled the room.

"Well, a hearing dog can hear the person's name being called, and will go get the deaf person and lead them to whoever is calling," explained Kathy. "I'm going to take off Rick's leash and call out Sue's name. Rick should run down and tap Sue and then bring her back to me. Do you want to see if he can do that?"

"Yes!" cried the kids.

"OK," said Kathy softly, "I need you all to be very quiet . . ." Kathy unsnapped Rick's leash and then called out loudly, "Sue! Sue! Sue!"

Rick knew just where Sue was. He leaped off the stage and ran back to where she was standing, jumped up against her lightly and then raced back through the crowd of kids. He took a mighty leap back up onto the stage and came to a sliding sit right at Kathy's feet. Sue followed a little less directly--she climbed the stairs at the side of the stage. Sue and Kathy both patted Rick as the kids called out happily and clapped for him. Rick turned to his audience wagging his tail. This was great!

Soon, Kathy and Sue gathered up all their things and walked the dogs back to the van. Each dog was given a big dog biscuit to chew on after they were back inside. Rick lay down to eat his treat and Susie curled up next to him with hers. They were both a little tired after their big performances.

Rick thought about all the children he had seen that day. At first he had been afraid they'd hurt him, but they hadn't. They petted him gently and clapped when he worked the sounds. The kids today weren't like Cynthia's grandchildren at all!

Chapter 16
Rick Goes to New York

"I sure hope this placement works out for Rick," said Jamie. "We're all a little worried about what Robin will be like."

Sue answered, "Well, when the interviewer went back to talk to her, she assured him that she really wanted a dog and would be willing to do all the work involved."

"Yeah, I know," replied Jamie. "But it still seems funny that her parents filled out her application and are the ones that answer our letters. I just hope for Rick's sake that she's OK."

"It's too bad Mrs. Scott isn't going to work out. I think she and Rick would have been great together," Sue said wistfully.

"Yeah," agreed Jamie. "Although, since she's less steady on her feet now, it makes sense for her to have a smaller dog that will be easier for her to work with and take care of."

"For her sake, I'm glad George persuaded her to go with a smaller dog, but now I'm awfully worried about Rick."

Sue looked down at the gray and black dog leaning against her legs and stroked his head, saying, "If this doesn't work out, Rick, you'll be out of the program." Sue ran her fingers through Rick's long hair, "I really think you could be a good hearing dog. I just wish you were going to someone we felt better about."

Jamie said, "Hey, look at the time. Are you ready to go to the airport?"

"Yeah, I think so," answered Sue. "Let's see; yes, I have my ticket and Rick's health certificate."

"What about dog food and some treats?"

Sue answered, "That stuff's all in my carry-on bag," as she patted the small bag hanging over her arm. "Well, we're ready when you are."

As Jamie opened the door of the training center, he said, "It's too bad Todd had to work this morning. I know he likes seeing you off."

"Yeah," answered Sue with a little smile.

Sue put Rick in the back of the van and then climbed in front with Jamie. Rick saw the big suitcase that Sue had taken on their earlier trip lying on the floor of the van. He wondered where they were going this time. He hoped it would be to a nice place.

Rick looked around the small room where he and Sue had slept. They had spent most of the previous day on an airplane, and Rick had been glad when late last night they had come here. He had been tired after the long flight and had gone to sleep immediately. It was only now that he began to wonder why they were here. Was Sue going to take him somewhere and leave him again? Since she had not left him last night, did that mean she would stay with him until they went home?

Rick felt a little apprehensive. He didn't want to be left with strange people again. He had just been getting used to living with Cynthia and Thomas when the kids started hurting him, and then Cynthia stopped wanting him to take her to sounds.

Rick thought back to when he was younger, growing up with his family. Those had been happy times. He had a big yard to play in, the children were kind to him, and he knew that he was loved. He wondered why his family had taken him to that place with all the cages and the loud barking dogs. He had gotten used to living at the training center and loved Sue and the other trainers, but he didn't feel as though he really belonged to anyone. He wished he could be like Annie and live with Sue.

"Are you ready to go outside?" Sue asked Rick. Rick walked to the door and sat while Sue snapped on his leash. She led him to a grassy area next to the parking lot and then opened the car door for him to jump in.

After driving a few minutes, Sue turned onto a long, curving driveway that wound through lots of tall, brick buildings. Finally, the car stopped in front of a building that looked just like others they had passed.

"OK Rick," Sue said, as she picked up his leash and held the back door open for him. Rick stepped out and looked around. "We're on a college campus, Rick. Robin is a student here and is supposed to live in this building. Let's see if we can find her." Sue added under her breath, "I sure hope this works out . . . "

Rick and Sue entered the brick building and walked down a very long hallway. They walked past many doorways before Sue finally stopped, saying, "Here it is, number 13." Sue pushed a button next to the door and they waited.

Suddenly, the door was opened wide by a young woman with dark curly hair. She stood looking at them for a moment and had a huge smile on her face. "You're here!" she said in a soft, rather high-pitched voice. "Come in, come in," she said, motioning them inside.

Rick and Sue walked into the small room. Sue unfastened the leash and then took off her coat. "This is your hearing dog, Rick," she said to Robin while moving her fingers. "What do you think of him?"

Robin sat down on the floor next to Rick. She looked at him for a moment and then gave him a big hug. "He's so beautiful," she said. "I'm so excited that he's finally here. I taped the picture you sent me of him on my wall. See? I have been looking at it every day."

Rick didn't mind being hugged by this new person. She seemed to know all the right places to pet him. As Robin stroked him softly on the head, Rick leaned toward her and closed his eyes.

"Well, you two seem to be getting along great!" said Sue, while signing to Robin. Rick looked up to see Sue smiling down at the two of them. "Why don't you show me your apartment and Rick's fenced yard, and then I'll leave you two alone for a few hours?"

"OK," said Robin, as she reluctantly got up from the floor. "Back here is the kitchen," she said, leading the way toward the back of the apartment, "and the bedroom and bathroom are down this hallway."

"Well, Rick won't have to look too far to find you," said Sue. "Small apartments make the dog's job pretty easy."

"Yeah, I can't really hide, can I?" said Robin with a laugh. "The college gave me special permission to build a little fenced area for Rick right behind the building. Do you want to go see it now?"

"Yes, let's go take a look. I'd like to make sure that the fence is high enough that Rick can't jump out."

The three went outside and walked down a little sidewalk running next to the edge of the building. Sue had started off holding Rick's leash but then motioned to Robin to stop, and handed it to her. "You might as well get started right now, OK?"

Sue turned to face Robin and began talking and moving both hands, now that she was no longer holding the leash. "Now, always make sure Rick's on your left side and hold onto the leash with your left hand about six inches from his collar." Sue moved Robin's hand down a little and said, "Yes, that's just right. Now walk ahead. If Rick lags behind, give him a little pull."

"Good," Sue said and motioned as Robin gave a tentative tug to Rick. Rick was trying to watch Sue, but she was now behind them. *Jerk* went the leash, and Rick hurried to keep up with Robin. He wanted to turn his head to see what Sue was doing but decided he'd better stay focused on Robin.

Sue had caught up with them now and signed and said, "Very good; now give him a pat."

Robin reached down and ruffled Rick's hair. "Good Boy," she said in her high voice. She pointed ahead saying, "There's his pen."

Rick and Sue saw a tall chain-link fence which enclosed a small area of grass. "That should be just fine, Robin," said Sue. "You should probably not leave him alone out here, though," Sue suggested, after noticing all the young children playing on the playground nearby. "One of the kids might open the gate and let him out."

"I'll always be out here to watch," promised Robin. "I wouldn't want anything to happen to Rick."

"Let's go back to your apartment and I'll give you some things to read about taking care of your hearing dog," said Sue. "Why don't you two walk back ahead of me? Try to keep him right next to your left leg as you go, and talk to him and pet him when he's heeling nicely."

"OK Rick, let's go," said Robin, giving him a gentle pull. "Come on." Rick had turned back to watch Sue, but now quickly hurried ahead with Robin.

Sue left soon after they had returned to the apartment, but somehow Rick didn't mind too much. Robin had sat with him on the floor in the living room and had petted him for a long time and told him how happy she was to have him.

Chapter 17
Robin, Rick and Randy

Sue had returned, and Rick lay happily next to her feet. He had missed her when she left, but Robin had been very nice to him and had kept him busy. The new woman had fed him, taken him for a walk, and then spent a long time brushing his hair.

"What's your class schedule this week?" Sue asked.

"I was able to get out of all of my classes except for my afternoon accounting class," answered Robin. "Will that be all right?"

"Yes, I'm sure that we can work around that," Sue answered. "By the way, are you planning to take Rick with you to your classes?"

"Well . . ." Robin started, "I thought I'd ask my professors if it's OK. I know that by law they have to let him come, and this being a deaf university they would be understanding, but I thought I'd just ask first."

"That's probably a good idea," Sue responded. "When you go to your accounting class this afternoon, why don't you ask your professor if Rick and I can both join you tomorrow?"

"Great!" exclaimed Robin. "I'm so excited about Rick; I just can't wait to show him off!"

Ring! Ring! Ring! A phone began to ring, a little lamp on the desk started to flash, and Rick jumped to his feet. Before he had time to get Sue, Robin picked up the receiver. Rick watched as Robin set the phone receiver on a machine and began typing, rather than talking. Rick could hear very faint sounds as she typed. He looked up at Sue.

"She's using a TDD, Rick," said Sue. "I know you don't understand, but that's one way deaf people can 'talk' to each other on the phone. They type messages back and forth instead of talking."

Eventually, Robin came back over to where Sue and Rick were sitting. "That was Randy," she said excitedly. "He wants to come over to see Rick."

"Who's Randy?" Sue signed.

"Oh! He's my fiancé," said Robin. "I can't wait for you to meet him."

Sue looked surprised. "I didn't know you were engaged! Are you planning to get married soon?"

"We would like to get married next month, if our loan is approved for the house we've been looking at," replied Robin.

"Oh dear," muttered Sue, "that sort of changes everything. You didn't mention wedding plans to George when he called to set up Rick's placement, did you?"

Robin answered, "No, I guess we did decide pretty suddenly; we've only been engaged a week. It's so exciting!"

"Well . . . I guess we should practice a few sounds before Randy gets here," Sue said with a sigh. "We can at least get Rick started working you."

Rick spent the next hour learning to tap Robin, instead of Sue, when he heard sounds. It didn't take him as long as with Cynthia, because he already knew what the game was. He also was getting to like Robin pretty well. She gave him treats when he tapped her for the sounds and often played with him, too.

Buzz! Buzzz! came a sound from the front door, and at the same time the overhead light began to flash. Rick had just taken Robin to the door a few minutes ago, but this time Sue wasn't outside ringing the bell. She was sitting next to Robin on the couch.

Rick hesitated and looked at Sue. Sue looked away. Rick then looked at Robin, who was sitting very still and kept glancing at him. That did it; Rick tapped Robin with his paw and then trotted over to the door. Robin told Rick what a good dog he was and then teased him with the tug-of-war. He grabbed it away and ran around the room.

Robin opened the front door and a young man with straight brown hair and freckles walked in. He hugged Robin and then crouched down and called to Rick.

Rick bounced over with his rag, wagging his tail.

"Do you want me to grab that?" asked Randy, while reaching for the tug-of-war. Rick let him have it and then waited intently for him to throw it. Suddenly, it flew across the room, and Rick chased after it. By the time Rick returned holding the soggy blue cloth he heard Sue talking.

"Hello," she said. "I'm Sue, Rick's trainer."

"Randy. Nice to meet you," Randy said to Sue as he signed to Robin. "Robin has been going crazy waiting for Rick to come. I'm glad you're here."

Robin motioned for everyone to sit down. She sat very close to Randy on the short couch, and Sue sat across from them in an easy chair with Rick lying at her feet,

"Robin tells me that you're planning to get married soon," said Sue.

"That's right," Randy answered. "We have been looking at a little house we'd like to buy, and if the bank decides to give us the loan, we'll get married and move right in."

"Are you working, or are you a student too?" Sue asked Randy while signing to Robin.

Robin answered, "He doesn't go here; he can hear." She laughed at her joke, and Randy joined in. "He graduated from the state university last year and is working here in town as a computer programmer."

"Actually, we met in Robin's computer class," Randy interrupted. "I was filling in for a sick professor, and she stayed after class to ask some questions . . and well . . ."

Sue asked Randy, "So you knew signing before you met Robin?"

"Yeah, My friend in high school was deaf, so I took some classes so I could talk to him. I've gotten lots of practice living here in Rochester, too. There are so many schools and colleges for the deaf that you run into lots of people who use sign language. You can even order a pizza by TDD."

"That's great," said Sue.

After glancing at the clock on the wall, Robin announced, "I have to go to class now, but you two are welcome to stay, if you'd like."

"Thanks," said Sue, "But I think I'll go back to the hotel for a while. I'll be back this evening so we can work some more."

"I think I'll just stay and get acquainted with Rick," Randy replied. Rick stood up and wagged his tail when Randy said his name.

Sue said slowly, "I'm sorry Randy, but it would probably be better if you didn't." She explained, "Until Rick has learned that he and Robin are a team, you shouldn't really spend much time with him."

Randy asked, "You mean Rick will get mixed up if I give him attention?"

"That's right. During the next few weeks, even months, Rick has to learn that he's to take Robin to sounds the way he's been trained to take me. It's easiest for the dog to learn that if he's only focusing on one person."

"You mean I shouldn't play with him or anything?" asked Randy.

"I'm afraid not. Eventually, when he and Robin have learned to work together, you can give him a little attention. But he will always have to be just Robin's dog."

"Oh," said Randy, looking hurt. "Well, OK. I guess I'd better leave too."

"Will Rick be all right by himself?" asked Robin.

"He'll be fine," answered Sue. "He'll wonder where we all have gone, but will then probably settle down and take a nap."

"Which one do you think Rick will like?" Robin asked Sue. They were standing in an aisle of a pet store looking at little plastic shapes wrapped in clear plastic and hanging on a wall. Rick was very interested in all the smells in this store. He caught a whiff of cats, of dogs, lots of kinds of food, and of something else that he couldn't identify.

"Why don't you let Rick pick?" Sue suggested. "Hold some toys that feel soft down where he can see them and squeak them a little."

"OK," said Robin. She picked a little duck, a monster with spines poking out all over, and a hot dog. *Squeeeak!* went the monster as she pressed on it. Rick looked up to see what she was doing. Oh! What's that? Rick sniffed all the packages but seemed most interested in the funny looking monster toy.

Robin said, "Do you like that one, Rick? OK, I'll get it for you." Turning to Sue she asked, "Does he need anything else?"

"Let's see . . . You have a training collar, food and water dishes, dog food, and some toys. Nope, that should be everything."

"How about a dog bed?" asked Robin.

"You can buy him a bed if you like," Sue answered, "but he'll be just as happy on a blanket or old cushion. Maybe you'll want to look around at home first."

Rick walked carefully next to Robin as they went to the front of the store to pay for his new things. He still wanted to keep an eye on Sue, but if he hesitated for long, Robin would give a pull on his leash. And, since Robin pet him and talked to him when he kept up with her, he chose to do just that.

Sue drove them back to Robin's apartment, and they all trooped in. Robin threw the bags she had been carrying onto the floor and sat down beside them.

"Let's see how you like your new toys," she said to Rick. Robin squeaked the little monster toy at Rick, and he danced with excitement. He wanted to grab that toy! Finally, Robin got the monster free of its wrapper and tossed it up in the air. Rick leaped up and caught the toy by its spines. As he happily chomped, it gave out little squeaks.

Robin next unwrapped a nylon toy shaped like a bone. Rick sniffed it. Yumm! It smelled like a real bone. He carried it off to the corner where he had left the monster and began chewing.

"Well, he likes them," said Robin. "I guess I'll have to keep checking at the store, so he can have new toys every once in a while."

Sue agreed, "It is a good idea to rotate his toys occasionally. And, adding new ones will keep him excited about working."

"Are we going with you to your accounting class today?" Sue asked.

"Actually, we're having a test today, so it wouldn't be much fun, but I did ask the prof about bringing Rick, and he said it's fine."

"Well, why don't we go tomorrow instead?" Sue suggested.

"OK," answered Robin. "Are you going to leave again for the afternoon?"

"Yes, but I think I'll make a call before I go." Sue signed again to Robin, "When did you say you would be hearing about the house?"

"Probably the end of the week," was the reply.

"Well, Why don't I call now and give you a chance to study a little before your test. I'll let myself out in a few minutes and be back this evening about seven."

"Great," said Robin. "I'll be looking for you then." Robin walked back to the bedroom and Rick followed halfway. He decided to lie in the hallway where he could keep an eye on both Sue and Robin.

"Hello, this is Sue," the trainer said into the phone. "I just wanted to call in and let you guys know how things are going."

"Oh, is he? Well, that's nice to hear . . . actually Rick's placement is going well, except that Robin is planning to get married next month and move . . .

"Yeah, she didn't even mention a boyfriend in her application, much less a fiancé. It seems everything has happened suddenly. He seems nice, but I'm not sure how much he's going to interfere with Rick. He walked in yesterday and started playing with him . . . "

"Yes . . . I explained everything to him . . . Well, we'll see."

"No, I haven't seen the house yet. I'm not even sure if it has a fenced yard or not. I'm mainly afraid that Rick is going to have so many changes during the next few weeks that he might get confused and stop working like he did at Cynthia's . . . "

"OK, I'll do my best," Sue said as she put down the phone. She gave a glance at Rick and then let herself out the front door.

That evening Sue came back and they practiced sounds for a while. Rick knew that he was doing well because Robin kept telling him what a good boy he was, and Sue looked very pleased. Finally, all three went into the living room to relax. Rick made himself comfortable on the soft, folded blanket that he had found next to the couch while Sue and Robin each sprawled across chairs.

"He's doing great!" said Robin.

"So are you," Sue said as she signed, "and the reason he's doing so well is because you've gained his trust. He knows you'll reward him when he's right, and correct him when he makes mistakes. It helps that you like him so well--dogs sure can tell."

"Well, Rick looks kind of worn out, so let's call it a day," suggested Sue, as she looked down at Rick who was lying on his blanket panting slightly. The trainer stood up and gave a little stretch. Rick watched Sue walk toward the door, but he felt too comfortable to get up and follow her. As Sue reached the door she turned and said, "I'll be back in the morning for our last day of training."

"This week has sure gone fast," Robin said. "And Rick is just so wonderful. He's woken me up every morning and hasn't missed a phone call yet. Say, when should I unplug my telephone light?"

Sue leaned an elbow against the door frame as she answered, "If you stay here, probably in a month or so. You only need it plugged in until you're sure he's working it every time."

"How about if we move?"

"Oh, Robin, I really don't know," answered Sue. "It's awfully hard on a dog to change things so soon. Often, people move a few years after they've had their dog, but you'll just have to be extra patient and see what happens. Actually, having the phone light will be a help while you're teaching him to answer your new phone there."

"How will he know where the new sounds are?" asked Robin in a concerned tone.

"You'll just have to teach them to him one by one, the way we've been doing this week," answered Sue. "Rick's a smart dog and you work well with him, so it should be fine." Sue continued, "What I'm most concerned about is having both a new person around and new sounds to learn."

"Oh, Sue," said Robin. "I can tell you're worried about this, but it'll be all right. Randy will do anything for me, and I know he'll be careful not to distract Rick . . . And, we may not even get the house, so Rick and I would stay right here."

"Yeah," said Sue, "I guess we shouldn't worry about moving until we find out for sure. But Robin, I think you should know the reason I'm especially uneasy about changing anything for Rick." Sue continued, "You see, this isn't his first placement. A few months ago I took him to a grandmother in Texas."

"Oh! I didn't know that," said Robin in a surprised tone. "What happened?"

"Well, it was really a mess," explained Sue. "Rick stopped working sounds for the woman after a few weeks and began taking her husband to sounds instead." Sue went on to tell Robin all about the Heralds.

"Oh dear," said Robin, "Poor Rick. She stretched out her foot and rubbed it gently across his back and asked. "Does this kind of thing happen very often?"

"No," answered Sue, "About ninety percent of the placements work out great. But once in a while we take a dog to someone who can't adjust to relying on a hearing dog or to a person who decides that it's too much work. Occasionally, we come across an allergy problem. Mostly though, we get enough information from a person's application and from their interview to decide who will be successful with a dog."

Sue shifted her position in the doorway and began leaning on her other elbow. "Anyway, it was a pretty confusing and unhappy experience for Rick. He bounced right back, though, when we started his training again, so we thought we'd give him one more chance."

"And this is it?" asked Robin.

"Yep," Sue answered. "This is it."

Chapter 18

A New Home

Robin and Rick practiced obedience and sounds all day with Sue. They were both trying very hard to learn everything that Sue wanted to teach them. Now it was evening and Rick was worn out. Earlier that day he had walked through a busy shopping center with Robin, practiced heeling, sitting and staying in a park, lain quietly beside Robin's chair in a restaurant while Sue and Robin ate lunch, and practiced every sound from every room in Robin's apartment.

As Rick lay resting on his soft blanket, he listened to Robin's and Sue's voices:

"When do you leave tomorrow?" asked Robin.

"My flight leaves at noon, so I'll probably go to the airport by 10," answered Sue. "I'm glad I'm not on the early flight that leaves at 6 a.m."

"We're going to miss you," Robin said. "I'll write as soon as we know about the house."

"I want you to write a lot. Rick's been a favorite of mine, and I'd like to hear everything that happens, not just the monthly progress reports."

"I'll write often," promised Robin. "And I'd like to hear about you and Todd, too. Do you think he'll ask you to marry him very soon?"

"We'll see," said Sue with a grin. "Anyway, I'll keep you posted."

Buzz! Buzz! Buzz! Rick bounced to attention and, as he was trotting over to Robin, he saw Sue glance at the door. Robin had kept talking and didn't stop until the overhead light began to flash. Rick had noticed this several times in the past few days. He also remembered this same thing happening at Cynthia's house. Sue would react when the phone, doorbell or oven timer sounded, but Cynthia never seemed to notice when sounds went off, unless she was looking at the flashing light.

Suddenly Rick thought he understood . . . Robin and Cynthia couldn't hear! They didn't look toward the sounds, because they couldn't hear them. Everything was making sense now. Rick had to touch Robin and take her to the door or the phone or to someone calling her name, because otherwise she wouldn't know that someone wanted to talk to her or that someone was at the door. Rick realized that he had been trained to listen for sounds so he could help someone who couldn't hear them. Wow! What an important job he had! Rick had been thinking hard but then realized that he should be working!

He expertly tapped Robin on her knee and then trotted over to the door and sat down. Robin patted Rick and dramatically pulled out the monster toy. She squeaked it at him and then tossed it down the hall. Rick ran to retrieve it. By the time he returned to the living room, Randy was there.

"Guess what?" Randy said excitedly while making big gestures with his hands. Without waiting for an answer he blurted out, "We got the loan! The house is ours!"

Randy grabbed Robin in a big hug, picked her up and swung her around. Rick thought that was exciting and stood up on his hind legs and began to bark. Randy then grabbed Rick's front paws and danced him around too. Everybody laughed.

Robin ruffled up Rick's hair. "We're going to move to a new house, Rick! You're going to love it."

Finally, the two excited people sat down on the couch.

"Congratulations!" said Sue. "I can tell you're really happy about this. Now you can start a life together."

"I can't wait," said Randy. "We've been wanting to get married, but I can't move into Robin's apartment here because I'm not a student, and the married student apartments are full."

"And Randy is just renting a very small room with an older couple," added Robin, "so that wouldn't work either."

"Well, that's settled now," said Sue. "How soon until you move?"

Randy answered, "The house is empty now, but it needs new wiring and stuff before we could actually live there. I talked to a contractor, and he said it will take about a month for all the repairs."

"So when's the wedding going to be?" Sue asked.

Robin said, "Gee, we'll have to decide all that, now that we got the house. I'm so excited!"

"I really ought to go," said Sue. "It's getting late, and I'm sure you two have a lot to talk about."

"Oh, come and look at the house," begged Robin.

"I'd like to, but it's already getting dark," Sue said. "Maybe I could take a quick look tomorrow morning before I leave. I really do want to see it."

"Let me write down the address for you," said Randy. "We can meet you there . . . When?"

"How about nine o'clock?" suggested Sue. "That should give me enough time to get to the airport."

"Great," said Robin. "You're just going to love it."

"Oh, I almost forgot," said Sue. "Does it have a fenced yard, or will you have to use Rick's portable pen?"

"The whole yard is fenced," answered Randy. "It will be perfect for Rick."

"OK, Until tomorrow then," said Sue, rising from her chair.

Rick happily explored the new place that Robin and Randy had brought him to. He thought it was strange that there was no furniture in the house, but it was fun running around through the empty rooms. Randy and Robin were busy measuring windows, so he eventually trotted out the back door, which was conveniently propped open, and investigated the yard.

Rick found an old doghouse under a big shady tree and discovered that it was just his size. As he settled down in the little house, he thought he smelled a bone. Yep, there it was in the corner. Rick decided that this was a very good place.

"Rick! Rick!" Robin called. "Guess who's here?"

Rick ran around to the front yard to see Sue just closing the front gate. He was happy to see his friend and rubbed against her legs.

"He seems to like it here," said Sue. "I can almost see a smile on his face."

"He's been out in the backyard," said Randy. "He found the old doghouse out there."

As they walked around to the back of the house, Sue said, "This yard is great, and the fence looks like it's in good shape too. Let's see inside."

Robin led the way into the house and the others all followed. After a short tour, Sue said she needed to get going.

"The house is perfect," Sue said as she looked around. "It's just the right size for you guys." As the trainer headed for the front door, she stopped and turned around. "You know, Robin, somehow I think the three of you are going to do just fine. I think this will work! Anyway, good luck with the wedding and everything, and let me know if you have any trouble teaching Rick the new sounds here."

The three of them walked her out to the front gate. Rick stood on his hind legs and rested his front paws on the gate so he could watch as Sue got into her car. Robin stood to one side of him, and Randy stood on the other.

Rick felt sad seeing Sue leave. He knew, somehow, that this time she wouldn't be coming back. Still, he felt fine staying with Robin. Rick knew that Robin loved him, but there was something else too . . . Robin **needed** him. Rick felt proud that he knew how to help to this kind young woman.

Sue called out, "Goodbye," and then her car pulled away. As Randy, Rick and Robin watched her leave, Rick felt Robin's hand on his head lightly stroking his soft gray hearing ears.

The End

Printed in Great Britain
by Amazon

20120458R00079